DARK PSYCHOLOGY

Psychology Facts You Should Know for the Best Results in Mind Hacking Process

(Mastery of Mind Control and Learning How to Influence People)

Leah Riggleman

Published by Sharon Lohan

© **Leah Riggleman**

All Rights Reserved

Dark Psychology: Psychology Facts You Should Know for the Best Results in Mind Hacking Process (Mastery of Mind Control and Learning How to Influence People)

ISBN 978-1-990334-53-5

All rights reserved. No part of this guide may be reproduced in any form without permission in writing from the publisher except in the case of brief quotations embodied in critical articles or reviews.

Legal & Disclaimer

The information contained in this book is not designed to replace or take the place of any form of medicine or professional medical advice. The information in this book has been provided for educational and entertainment purposes only.

The information contained in this book has been compiled from sources deemed reliable, and it is accurate to the best of the Author's knowledge; however, the Author cannot guarantee its accuracy and validity and cannot be held liable for any errors or omissions. Changes are periodically made to this book. You must consult your doctor or get professional medical advice before using any of the suggested remedies, techniques, or information in this book.

Upon using the information contained in this book, you agree to hold harmless the Author from and against any damages, costs, and expenses, including any legal fees potentially resulting from the application of any of the information provided by this guide. This disclaimer applies to any damages or injury caused by the use and application, whether directly or indirectly, of any advice or information presented, whether for breach of contract, tort, negligence, personal injury, criminal intent, or under any other cause of action.

You agree to accept all risks of using the information presented inside this book. You need to consult a professional medical practitioner in order to ensure you are both able and healthy enough to participate in this program.

Table of Contents

INTRODUCTION 1

CHAPTER 1: THE HISTORY OF NEURO-LINGUISTIC PROGRAMMING (NLP) 13

CHAPTER 2: HISTORY OF PERSUASION AND MANIPULATION 28

CHAPTER 3: THE DARK SIDE OF PSYCHOLOGY 46

CHAPTER 4: UNDERSTAND THE 4 PERSONALITY TRAITS OF THE DARK TRIAD 49

CHAPTER 5: IDENTIFYING RED FLAGS: IDENTIFYING PSYCHOPATHS, SOCIOPATHS, MACHIAVELLIANS, AND NARCISSISTS 65

CHAPTER 6: THE ART OF PERSUASION 75

CHAPTER 7: DIFFERENT TYPES OF DARK PSYCHOLOGY AND MANIPULATION TACTICS 89

CHAPTER 8: POWERFUL COMMUNICATION TECHNIQUES 100

CHAPTER 9: STEP BY STEP INSTRUCTIONS TO VIABLY PLANT A THOUGHT INTO THE PSYCHES OF OTHER INDIVIDUALS 117

CHAPTER 10: DARK MANIPULATION TECHNIQUES 138

CHAPTER 11: MYTHS AND MISCONCEPTIONS ABOUT DARK PSYCHOLOGY 150

CHAPTER 12: HOW TO USE DARK PSYCHOLOGY AND MANIPULATION IN DAILY LIFE 167

CHAPTER 13: THE TECHNIQUES USED IN DARK PERSUASION 171

CONCLUSION 187

Introduction

Psychology is going to underpin everything in our lives from advertising to finance, crime to religion, and even from hate to love. Someone who can understand these psychological principles is someone who holds onto the key to human influence.

This is not an easy task, which is why most people don't possess it. Learning all of the different principles of psychology is not necessary. Start with the lessons in these pages, and you'll have a solid foundation. You have to be able to read people, understand what makes them tick, and understand why they may react in ways that may not be normally expected. And even then, you may need to spend time taking classes and reading through countless books to gain a complete understanding. It depends how far you want to go with this.

So, if only a few people understand psychology and how the human mind works, why is it so important to know what this is? It is because those who do know what it is and how to use it can choose to use that power and that knowledge against you.

How Dark Psychology Is Used Today?

While some people are going to use these dark psychology tactics to harm their victim, there are times when you may use these tactics without the intent of negatively manipulating another person. Some of these tactics were either unintentionally or intentionally added to our toolbox from a variety of means that could include:

When you were a child, you would see how adults, especially those close to you, behaved.

When you were a teenager, the mind and your ability to understand the behaviors around you were expanded truly.

You were able to watch others use the tactics and then succeed.

Using the tactics may have been unintentional in the beginning, but when you found that it worked to get you what you wanted, you would start to use those tactics intentionally.

Some people, such as a politician, a public speaker, or a salesperson, would be trained to use these types of tactics to get what they want.

Dark Psychology Tactics That Are Used regularly

Love flooding: This would include any buttering up, praising, or complimenting people to get them to comply with the request that you want. If you want someone to help you move some items into your home, you may use love flooding to make them feel good, which could make it more likely that they will help you. A dark manipulator could also use it to make the other person feel attached to them and then get them to do things that they may not normally do.

Lying: This would include telling the victim an untrue version of the situation. It can also include a partial truth or exaggerations to get what you wanted to be done.

Love denial: This one can be hard on the victim because it can make them feel lost and abandoned by the manipulator. This one includes withholding affection and love until you can get what you want out of the victim.

Withdrawal: This would be when the victim is given the silent treatment or is avoided until they meet the needs of the other person.

Restricting choices: The manipulator may give their victim access to some choices, but they do this to distract them from the choices that they don't want the victim to make.

Semantic manipulation: This is a technique where the manipulator is going to use some commonly known words, ones that have accepted meanings by both parties, in a conversation. But then they will tell the victim, later on, that they had meant something completely different when they used that word. The new meaning is often going to change up the entire definition and could make it so that the conversation goes the way the manipulator wanted, even though the victim was tricked.

Reverse psychology: This is when you tell someone to do something in one manner, knowing that they will do the opposite. But the opposite action is what the manipulator wanted to happen in the first place.

Who Will Deliberately Use Dark Tactics?

Many different people may choose to use these dark tactics against you. They can be found in many different aspects of your life, which is why it is so important to learn how to stay away from them. Some of the people who can use some of these dark psychology tactics deliberately include:

Narcissists: These individuals are going to have a bloated sense of their self-worth, and they will need to make others believe that they are superior as well. To meet their desires of being worshipped and adored by everyone they meet, they will use persuasion and dark psychology.

Sociopaths: Those who are sociopaths are charming, intelligent, and persuasive. But they only act this way to get what they want. They lack any emotions, and they are not able to feel any remorse. This means that they have no issue with using the tactics of dark psychology to get what they want, including taking it as far as creating superficial relationships.

Politicians: With the help of dark psychology, a politician could convince someone to cast votes for them simply by convincing these people that their point of view is the right one.

Salespeople: Not all salespeople are going to use dark tactics against you. But it is possible that some, especially those who are really into getting their sales numbers and being the best, will not think twice about using dark persuasion to manipulate people.

Leaders: Throughout history, there have been plenty of leaders who will use the techniques of dark psychology to get their team members, subordinates, and citizens do what they want.

Selfish people: This could be any person that you come across who will make sure that their own needs are put before anyone else's. They aren't concerned about others, and they will let others forego their benefits so that they can benefit. If the situation benefits them, it is fine if it benefits someone else. But if someone is going to be the loser, it will be the other person and not them.

This list is important because it is going to serve two purposes. First, it is going to help you be more aware of the people who may try to manipulate you to do things that you don't want to do, and it can be there to help out with self-realization.

Wide, Practical and Theoretical observations

Murder, rape, incest, abuse, all words that can send chills up your spine. As a culture we have saturated ourselves with negative ideals for entertainment purposes. We sit and watch horror movies, crime shows, and reality shows diving into the minds of the deviant. The darkness within these becomes an obsession for some, and though they don't reenact or find the actions preferable, there is a connection that few want to recognize outwardly. While the majority of human beings have a buffer in their mind, knowing fact from fiction and right from wrong, some lack it.

Imagination is one thing. Combing through the worst fears of people to find what scenario can be the scariest and most grabbing is something that fiction writers and creators do. Often though, when watching these dark psyches at work on the screen in front of you, the human mind finds certain recognition of why the predator or villain did what they did. Some movies and books even prey on the idea of the worst human condition. Depraved and distraught, the father who witnessed his family's murders climbs out of his ominous depression to wreak havoc on those that committed the acts to begin with. There is a satisfaction for people in the revenge of heinous acts. But then, doesn't that apply the same dark psyche to the perpetrator, regardless of the reasoning behind it?

Dark Psychology has no pointed targets and cares little for the reasoning behind the actions. It is the actual act of manipulation, deceit, and harm that carries the weight within the dark psyche. The idea of revenge has been around a very long time, and at some significant points in history was considered a requirement of honor if wrong was done to you. Very clear examples of the "eye for an eye" concept are still in existence today. The death penalty is one such example, though the root of it is wide and doesn't currently encourage private actions of one person to another. The federal organization as a whole is in charge of carrying out the punishment. But long before that, laws were erected in civilizations that based themselves on the idea of revenge.

The Code of Hammurabi

The Code of Hammurabi dates back to Babylonian times. Around 1760 B.C., the king of Babylon set forth a stone pillar inscribed with the laws of his kingdom. They are considered to be the oldest discovered set of laws in our history as human beings. What is so significant about the Code of Hammurabi? It is the fact that it is set in the pure idea of revenge. King Hammurabi believed wholeheartedly in the idea of an eye for an eye and set forth over thirty laws of Babylonia based on that specific theory.

Through time, this code has shown its influence through almost all judicial and legal systems. Even the American justice system is predicated on the idea of an eye for an eye. A punishment system where retribution for a crime is equal in severity to the crime committed. What was not expected or understood was the fact that this revenge system is actually, internally governed by a specific part of our brains called the dorsal striatum. This sector controls the idea of revenge within our minds. For victims of crime, the dorsal striatum is more active. So ultimately, with a society of an eye for an eye, we are taking the actions of a dark psyche and melding a new one from their actions.

One very prominent case of revenge on a large scale would be the St. Bartholomew's Day Massacre. This massacre occurred during the Protestant Reformation in the sixteenth century. During this time, a new sect of Christianity had been created, and the Catholic Church stood to lose control and power over people, land, and money. In August of 1572 the French Protestants flooded Paris for the marriage of a Catholic woman to a Protestant aristocrat. When the wedding was over, King Charles IX ordered that the aristocrat be killed for his crimes to the church. To make it as easy as possible, he also ordered the murder of the Protestants within the town and then outward into the French countryside. That case of revenge cost society between thousand and four thousand lives.

Chapter 1: The History Of Neuro-Linguistic Programming (Nlp)

The point of NLP is to aid the user in learning how their (or their subject's) mind interprets and processes words (linguistics). NLP consists of numerous working components—namely, techniques and strategies for achieving excellence and success through understanding how our thoughts and behavior influences outcomes. Richard Bandler himself defined NLP as: "... An attitude which is an insatiable curiosity about human beings with a methodology which leaves behind it a trail of techniques." John Grinder, the co-founder of NLP, similarly defined it as: "The strategies, tools and techniques... [which] represent an opportunity unlike any other for the exploration of human functioning, or more precisely, that rare and valuable subset of human functioning known as genius" (Nlp.com, 2020).

Historically, many ideologies played a role in the formation of NLP. Cybernetics, the study of communication and automatic control systems, contributed largely to the kind of thinking that laid the path for the birth of NLP. Cybernetics is the area of study from which NLP draws its notion of a "closed signaling loop"—this relationship became apparent when John Grinder, one of the founding fathers of NLP, stated that: "the basic unit of analysis in face-to-face communication is the feedback loop." It essentially concerns itself with the study of learning, cognition, adaptation, social control, emergence, convergence, communication, efficacy, and connectivity. The word 'cybernetics' has Greek etymology, with the original Greek root word meaning 'governance.' The word itself first appeared in Plato's Alcibiades (Sciencedirect.com, 2020).

The early twentieth century saw a "self-help" wave sweep over America. This was perhaps the greatest push towards using NLP to make changes in one's personal life, instead of just using it as a management tool within a business or to help kick a habit like smoking. The stage was set for Grinder and Bandler by books like Dale Carnegie's How to Win Friends and Influence People, first published in 1936, and Norman Vincent Peale's The Power of Positive Thinking, first published in 1952.

Maslow's hierarchy of needs, initially published in his paper, A Theory of Human Motivation, is a theory of psychological well-being built on fulfilling innate human needs in priority, culminating in self-actualization. In 1943, Maslow stated that men whose entire hierarchy of needs had been met would be as close to perfection (and capable of contemplating deeper things) as humanly possible. Maslow also believed in 'modeling,' a concept which will be further covered in the next chapter.

In NLP, modeling refers to when one takes on the characteristics of a more successful person in hopes of becoming more successful themselves. Maslow modeled up to sixty people whom he believed to be self-realized at the time. Modeling was not just for the average Joe, however. The founding fathers of NLP, John Grinder and Richard Bandler, modeled themselves after three psychology professionals whom they had admired: Fritz Perls and his signature work around Gestalt therapy, Virginia Satir and her Systemic Family Therapy, and Milton Erickson's Hypnotherapy. This admiration grew and grew until it eventually bloomed into NLP itself.

Grinder and Bandler often questioned how these specialities could be used by others, as well. First, they considered the communication patterns used, then their attitudes, and finally, the psychotherapist's unique perspective was taken into account.

Fritz Perls, a German-born psychiatrist who mainly treated patients using Gestalt therapy, focused on enhancing awareness of sensation, perception, emotion, behavior, and teaching personal responsibility. This humanistic form of psychotherapy aimed to enable the recipient to become more creative and fully alive. Gestalt therapy was at its peak during the mid-twentieth century, and still holds strong even today. It remains a popular choice of treatment for mental health patients and those in need of counseling.

On the other hand, Virginia Satir, the pioneer of Systemic Family Therapy, focused on families or 'groups' rather than on a singular individual and their problems and challenges. Systemic Family Therapy differs from more traditional forms of therapy since it doesn't examine the underlying causes to problems within a relationship. Instead, it seeks to correct how people choose to approach these problems. Satir isn't the only American psychotherapist whose therapies have been absorbed into the core tenets of NLP—it is important not to forget the contributions and writings of Milton Erickson.

Erickson's hypnotherapy aims to increase both a person's focus and their suggestibility by inducing a trance-like state. But this hypnotherapy was unique—it was language-centered, and it earned its own name: Ericksonian hypnotherapy. The complex language patterns Erickson employed during therapy were in direct contrast to the informal conversational style which he otherwise used when conversing with his patients. The divergence from swinging a pocket watch in front of a Victorian damsel's face to wordplay led many of Erickson's colleagues to shun him. Erickson must have often been told that he was a fraud, with many remaining skeptical of his theories and ideas during his academic lifetime.

While Bandler and Grinder's contemporaries were notable, the true birth of NLP happened at the University of California in Santa Cruz, where Grinder had been studying psychology and Bandler had been lecturing on linguistics. At the time, Bandler had been carrying out an in-depth study on Satir, and noticed something strange. He realized that certain phrases and questions employed by Satir had proven effective in eliciting a desired response from her patients. By this time, both Bandler and Grinder had already met and were working together. Bandler quickly pulled Grinder into his world, asking for his help researching why Satir, and her magical language, had been so therapeutic and healing to severely disturbed patients and incredibly strained relationships alike. The result of this research can be deemed as the infancy of NLP.

NLP is not a theoretical set of concepts; rather, it is a series of 'models.' These models are perspectives that allow for predictions.

NLP also functions on a set number of presuppositions. Although numerous NLP authors have differing lists of tenements, the core values are:

• That verbal communication is, to put it bluntly, largely pointless. What is meant by this is that the words employed in conversation are often one of the least important cues to look out for. Studies have found that in emotional situations, about 90% of communication is non-verbal. NLP thus encourages one to place equal focus on the tone of voice, rhythm, pauses in speech, facial expressions, and body language.

- The only point of communication is the response it elicits. Someone who is mindful of NLP is more concerned with how their communicative partner responds to this communication than with the communication itself. This creates somewhat of a moral gray area because, in this case, truthfulness may come second to what needs to be said in order to draw out the wanted reaction.

- People exist within their own 'map' of reality. For example, it is considered ill-mannered in America to eat with your hands in a formal setting, however, in some regions of Japan, it is considered a compliment. Despite all living in the same world, our experiences are subjective. We attach meaning to words, places, people, music, and art which to others might be entirely meaningless. Understanding someone's world map is essentially understanding them, and thus offers insight into how to communicate with them more efficiently.

• All people are influenceable through NLP. This is true simply because all people live within these maps of reality, instead of reality itself. This subjective view of the world is ever changing, which makes it manipulatable. By changing someone's map of reality, you essentially alter any future responses they may have to any stimuli. To fail is to learn. There is a famous story about a reporter who visited Thomas Edison at his homestead. This surly reporter, instead of praising Edison, asked him how it felt to have failed 10,000 times before inventing the lightbulb. Edison glibly replied that he had not failed 10,ooo times, but had learned on 10,000 occasions how not to make a lightbulb. This same approach should be taken with

NLP. You will not always elicit the sought-after response on your first try, but don't view this as a loss. View it as a gain, as you will have gained insight into the person's map of reality.

● The importance of choice. The person with whom you're communicating using NLP techniques needs to feel that they have a choice, even if this is just an illusion. When faced with no way out or no way of refusing, people become aggressive and difficult to work with. By offering this person a choice, you ensure they have a say in their own destiny—they do not realize that both alternatives are outcomes which you desire.

● Breaking things into bite-sized chunks. If you're hoping to elicit a big response from someone (for example, getting them to stop smoking), it's best not to face the main challenge immediately. For instance, it would be best to start pointing out to the person how horrible smoking smells, or how yellow their fingertips have become, before suggesting that they should give up the habit entirely. During these tiny 'nudges' toward the end goal, one can observe the person'sreactions to determine which way would be best to influence them.

Robert Dilts published his most well-known book, Neurological Levels, in 1990. This essentially changed the way that NLP was, and still is, approached. In this book, Dilts set out various neurological levels upon which a person may operate, and the various corresponding levels of motivation connected to the aforementioned neurological levels. These levels and their unique motivations are:

● Identity: What kind of person is the recipient motivated to become? What kind of person do they believe themselves to currently be?

● Spirit: Is the person motivated to do morally good things? Do they follow any specific religious path which may inhibit or motivate the way in which they act?

- Capability: What is the recipient capable of doing? Is what you're asking the recipient within the realm of possibility? If not, what incapacitates the person from doing the aforementioned?

In this case, identity is the most important neurological level, according to Dilts—the theory being that if you are capable of motivating someone through identity, nearly any suggestion should be successful (as long as it remains within the realm of possibility).

NLP believes that human beings are somewhat like computers in the sense that all behaviors are direct results of sensory information and processes. It is for this reason that familiarity with "well-formedness conditions" is important to NLP practitioners. Well-formedness conditions are established patterns of behavior, things that we do regularly. Driving home from work is thus a well-formedness condition, but so is that warm, fuzzy feeling you have inside when having a heart-to-heart with an old friend.

Behavior does not have to be physically manifested. It is important to remember this. Emotional behavior is considered behavior too, in the field of psychotherapy.

Grinder and Bandler also emphasize the idea of ecology. An NLP practitioner needs to be aware of the effect his or her actions may have, before making a change in the NLP recipient. It is important to consider how this change will affect their personal relationships, their professional relationships, their financial security, and their overall quality of life.

Grinder and Bandler believed that people, like computers, had pre-programmed "meta-programs." They hypothesized that one needed to be familiar with someone's meta-programs in order to access their perspective. These meta-programs represent biases within a person's behavioral processing system, and include things such as whether or not someone prioritizes by considering the short-term or the long-term consequences, and their intrinsic and extrinsic motivations—are they motivated by moving toward positive outcomes, or by steering clear of negative outcomes, generalities or details. It also includes their sense of introversion versus extroversion, whether they focus on similarities or differences, and what is their preferred context for information (whether this centres around people, procedures, places, actions, or emotions).

NLP originally developed in four distinctive waves known as: NLPure, NLPt, NLPeace, and NLPsych (Rogozinska, 2016).

NLPure refers to the original wave of NLP that swept over the globe after being unleashed upon us by Bandler and Grinder. To be more specific, NLPure first surfaced in 1972, after the release of Bandler and Grinder's paper titled Success and Enthusiasm. Success and Enthusiasm saw the birth of NLP. NLPure is NLP in its most basic, elementary form, as originally envisaged by Grinder and Bandler.

NLPt emerged in 1989 through another one of Dilts's novels: Health and Joy of Living. It is, in essence, the second wave of NLP, as developed from Grinder and Bandler's earlier theories. 1995 saw the founding of the European Association of Neuro-Linguistic Programming Training (EANLPt).

NLPeace was the next phase. It was born out of the spiritual movement of the 1990s and largely inspired by another of Dilts's novels, Spirituality and the Meaning of Life.

NLPsych is the fourth, and thus far final, wave of NLP. The Research and Recognition Project crafted and honed NLPsych into what it is today. The idea of NLPsych was to give NLP counselors a way to receive professional accreditation for the therapy, offered in the form of a certified degree called NPsych.

Chapter 2: History Of Persuasion And Manipulation

Persuasion is one of the fundamental skills for all professionals. Regardless of profession and function. In addition, we all like, want, and need to be understood and understood. And many times, we need supporters for our ideas and actions. Persuasion is aligned with the ability to influence people and convince them of something. For psychologist Robert Cialdini, one of the greatest authorities on the subject: Persuasion is the ability to bring people to our side. To do that, just change the way we present our arguments. Furthermore, research shows that emotionally intelligent, happy, and successful people have a high capacity to persuade, influence, sell, negotiate, motivate, and understand human nature.

Unfortunately, most people face moments when they don't get what they are looking for. However, this is not a reason to believe that we are not capable but rather a sign that we need and can improve the skills of persuasion and influence. In practice, there are not many differences between one and the other. Persuasion is something more incisive and direct, whether in a negotiation or sale, for example. The influence is more natural and intrinsic, built on a daily basis. The main traits and characteristics of persuasive professionals are updating, honesty, organization, good listener, hardworking, proactive, humble, creativity, determination, confidence, and the ability to understand behavior. Furthermore, the main skills of persuasive and prosperous people are empathy, trust, authority, communication, and self-motivation. Empathy is the ability to understand the other, to see situations from their perspective.

Above all, feeling what she feels and worrying about meeting her needs. The best persuaders notice and know what the other person feels and can connect with them in 30 seconds or less. This is for two interesting reasons. The first one is due to their excellent perception. The second, because human behavior is predictable. There are certain triggers or automatic reactions common to anyone.

While mistrust today permeates people's minds, persuasion experts have the ability to trust. If we are to persuade, we need to establish trust. Untrustworthy people react defensively, are not sincere, avoid advice, blame others, and repeat defeatist habits. Mainly, authority is another ability of persuasion. It shows who you are in terms of your specialty or your business, your background, what accredits you to other people or professionals. The best persuaders have authority and are respected. Respect is achieved little by little through conduct in personal and professional matters. If you are a respected person with integrity and character in all aspects, business, career, and leadership, people will know and respect you for that.

Communication and self-motivation are other essential skills for a persuader of excellence. Both to establish a connection with people and to show confidence and motivation in relation to what you want to defend, sell, or negotiate. If during this reading, I managed to arouse curiosity about the topic, convince you that persuasion is an important skill and that it must be improved, it is because I was able to persuade you using the appropriate techniques. If people can answer questions that solve global problems, how can they persuade others to believe otherwise? From friendly discussions to continental warfare, one person will always have a different opinion than the other. So there is no controversy if we ever force people to look at the eye level. Of course, empirical studies of persuasion and elimination still lack such omnipotent insights. However, research has grown and evolved rapidly over the past 70 years. Psychological research on beliefs has become one of the most influential endeavors of our time, with knowledge affecting political propaganda and public moral marketing strategies. Empirical research on this topic did not begin until the Second World War, where it is important to understand how people's views are affected.

The economy was already struggling, and the disagreement between the classes was so great that the country promised to enter into a long and protracted war. To persuade people to support this cause, the government recognized the need for expert advice. The government examined how the Ministry of War Information and the Ministry of Education's finances impacted on the quality of the source of persuasive news, the content of the message, and the attitude of the recipients—recruited prominent social psychologists across the country. Based on this persuasive research, the public flyer was quickly framed with arguments on both sides (not one page).

In soldier orientation film, men recite according to section. In fact, the results of this project have helped to create one of the nation's greatest efforts to influence public opinion. After the war, all researchers returned to their facilities, and some followers independently analyzed the mental processes underlying beliefs. In the following decades, they have expanded our understanding of how others and our environment can change our beliefs. However, as research drew to a close in the 1980s, curious interpretations of science emerged. Some studies have shown a diversion effect, while others now show the opposite effect. For example, the benefits of bilateral messages recorded in previous studies have now been reversed in subsequent studies.

As a result, many psychologists have begun to lose hope in this area, and have declared that studying beliefs is a waste of scientific effort. But that changes when a year later, two rebel graduate students discover a psychological theory that combines everything between persuasion and manipulation.

The persuasion, trigger tricks, and techniques are not new - they have been used for a long time. Aristotle's rhetoric was one of the earliest works on persuasion techniques 2000 years ago. The guiding methods presented by Aristotle are ethics (authenticity), logos (reasons), and pathos (emotions). We also discussed the importance of gyroscope (random time) for the simulation method. Today, stimulating methods for advertising, marketing, and communication are used around us. We convince when we try to convince the next person of the overview or to win the next design customer or the next project. The influence of Robert Chardini when Aristotle first documented coercion: motivational psychology is often mentioned when talking about modern coercion. According to Cialdini, persuasion has six main principles.

Phase

People are forced to give something back in order to receive something.

Defect

People love what can keep them down.

Makes

People follow the path of trustworthy and knowledgeable professionals.

Consistency

People want to agree with what they said and did before.

Preference

People want to say yes to those who want it.

Consensus (social evidence)

Especially when they are unsure, people decide what to do by looking at the actions and actions of others. We are all exposed to one or more of these guidelines and can identify them when we advertise or interact with other users. This has been the case for years, but the application of leading technology to new technologies and media is relatively new.

It started with a personal computer, is very popular on the Internet and is now widely used on mobile devices.

Inspired by technology and new media

Behavioral researcher PJ Bock is a pioneer in studying the role of technology in stimulation. Twenty years ago, he began to explore the interplay between constraint and computer technology. This includes websites, software, devices, and other interactive technologies that are used to change people's attitudes and behaviors. He called this field captology an abstract technology based on computers and wrote a book that uses our compelling technology: computers to change our thinking and behavior.

Captology is a shadow area where computer technology and stimulus overlap. Captology describes the overlap between shaded areas and stimuli in computer technology (developed from BJ Folks CHI 98 paper that triggers the computer). (Large preview)

Interactive technology has many advantages over traditional media because it is interactive. It is also permanent (e.g., reminders of software updates), anonymous (ideal for important topics), access to and processing of large amounts of data (e.g., recommendations from Amazon) as well as many styles and methods (text, graphics). Audio, video, animation, simulation), easy to scale, and widely used. This last advantage is even more pronounced today as cell phones are an extension of our hands, and the proliferation of smart devices, embedded computing, IoT, wearable technology, augmented reality, virtual reality, and AI-enabled virtual assistants are increasing. Everything around us. In addition, today's technological advances allow users to know their location, environment, time, and routines, which enables longer tripping times and target moments. This can remind you to get up from your smartwatch and move around or offer in a cafe when you're a few blocks away.

Ethics And New Technology And Interactive Media

The use of persuasion in traditional media over the past decades has raised questions about the ethical use of persuasion. With new media and pervasive technology, there are more questions about the ethical use of persuasion, some of which are due to the advantages pervasive technology has over traditional media and humans. Anyone using persuasive methods to change people's minds or behavior should have a thorough understanding of the ethical implications and impact of their work. One of the major tasks of a designer in the design process is to be a user advocate. This role is even more important when stimulus techniques are deliberately used in the design because they cannot be used for tricks that persuade users. To make matters worse, some users may not be aware of this trick. This is for children, the elderly, or other vulnerable users.BJ Folk offers six factors in convincing users that interactive technology works better than users.

Authentic intentions are overshadowed by novelty

The web and email are no longer new, and most of us have misunderstood the web practices and the promise of the Nigerian prince, but new mobile applications, voice interfaces, AR, and VR are still new. Not too long ago.

New technology is popular

"This must be true — I saw it on the Internet" is now a punchline, but users still want fake news and bot-generated content to visualize, comment, share, retweet, distribute and disseminate.

Unlimited tolerance

Should a used car dealer follow you after your first visit and try to sell you a car? Fortunately, this is not really the case, but apps and devices are always with you, and the brightening and shining screens keep us in the wrong place or time. You can trust them forever. In the past, my son retired from his mobile device. When he launched it after Easter, he received hundreds of previous announcements and warnings from cellphone games, which provided all sorts of reminders and incentives to use it again.

Control how interactions develop

Contrary to the human belief that optimists can react and change course, this technology has pre-defined options controlled by developers, designers, and developers. When designing a language interface, teachers must define what they can do with their skills; otherwise, "Sorry, I can't help you." Last month, social networks blocked access to mobile websites and asked them to install apps to access content without the option of escape or release.

Emotions can affect them before they occur

There is no passion for new technology. Despite recent advances in artificial intelligence, machines do not feel like humans. Going to the Google Duplex Assistant call mentioned at the outset, it treats someone else if the user does not know that the other person's voice is just a numbing machine.

Cannot be held responsible for the negative effects of trust

What if something goes wrong, and the application of technology cannot be held responsible? If the stimulus strategy had unintended consequences or was abused by a partner, is the author responsible? Mark Zuckerberg is responsible for the Cambridge Analytica scandal before and after congressional hearings.

In the light of these unfair advantages, how do we, as creators, designers, and developers, make ethical decisions about our designs and solutions? On the one hand, step back and look at the ethical implications and implications of our work. User Levels Here: Many designers refuse to speak out loud about the ethical questioning of technical products and designs. Former Google design ethicist Tristan Harris talks about how technology companies can attract users. Sean Parker, founder of Napster and former president of Facebook, explained how Facebook was created using human "vulnerabilities." Moreover, BaseCamp's Jonas Downey considers how most software products are owned and operated by companies that often conflict with user interests.

All operational arguments for non-compliance consist of a few examples in which persuaders are manipulated to maintain a mental framework based on the performance of actions. Exclusive persuader is treated under conditions that are sufficient for compliance persuader to act independently. One such example, used in a compliance breach debate, expresses the intuition that the agent is not acting freely due to the extensive nature of the operation and is not morally responsible for what she does.

It has to be done. It is said that persuaders who go through the crucial process and get into the same state of mind make no difference to the proper operation in each case. It was therefore concluded that the appropriate conditions for the free will and moral responsibility proposed by the applicant were insufficient and that freedom and moral obligation were incompatible with the resolution. One way in which compliance officers oppose the debate about certain operations is to refer to the historical needs that they are addressing, and that is not the relevant manipulator. Since many conservatives have submitted historical papers, this study shows that prehistoric views still have a life to protect non-historical conservatives like Harry Frankfurt. I double my efforts. Historic conformists are ashamed not to trust illegitimate conformal rivals.

These terms seem to be the opposite, the stimulus acts as a form of "honest" action, and the actor is at the forefront of his goals and ideas. For the purposes of this book, however, it is more meaningful to consider stimulation as a step in the process.

Persuasion is a process that becomes manipulation. Low performance is one of the controls. How many times have you discussed with someone else to raise your hand and say "absolutely perfect"? You can count these events on the other hand. It may be easy to convince someone that smoking is unhealthy, but is it easy to force them to quit? In such cases, the government does not recognize the need and benefits of higher taxes to prevent the use of tobacco products. As defined in this book, the government deals with tobacco use and attempts to achieve this goal using a number of methods, including coercion.

What about the other influence? And other operating modes? Well, the function needs to be intentional and have some kind of goal — that goal is just to create confusion. A great filmmaker can influence many other works, but this is very different from the process. Filmmakers do not want to affect others (even if they want to), but they do so through the reactions of others in their work.

Persuasion is not the only functional mode that can be used. A simple alternative is a lie and a type of fraud. To be able to believe and be trusted is to change the perception of those who believe. As mentioned earlier, success is still a function. Beliefs and influences are not affected by image issues such as functions. In fact, being able to hold a "convincing argument" is considered positive. Although it has a creepy glitter; The phrase "I am very confident" refers to the power to exercise power over other parties. When an employer refers to a "firm" soft ability, it is appropriate to interpret this as an e-song representation of the process at least partially.

Chapter 3: The Dark Side Of Psychology

Our body has such function as self-regulation of all physiological procedures, to put it simply, brain reactions on the change in the chemical processes in the body.

Probably, under the influence of emotions in the body happens some kind of change, for instance, in blood composition, then it is sent to the brain, and again the reaction impulse from the brain is transmitted to one of the organs and thus pain occurs. This is called the psychological reason for the strong pain.

For instance, when you fear darkness you could experience heartache or discomfort in the throat. You feel like someone stops your breathing. Here you fear not darkness itself but something that can be there in the darkness. It is based on gotten information about it during your life. A kid never fears the darkness till she or he is being told what can be in it. Let us call it conscious fear.

Such phobias as fear of a concrete situation or item, that terrifies you with something and creates some feeling of fear and horror, are also described as mindful fear since you feel this fear just because of your disappointment or negative information gotten from another person. What is the nature of this fear? How does this fear happen? What do I feel? Uncertainty, humiliation, rejection, inactivity, anxiety, blame, injury, consternation, tension, and panic.

There are psychological and physical experiences in your body. And this means that fear is interconnected with other negative feelings. Just one thing triggers another, and comes from the other, but means one and the exact same thing.

What about unconscious fear or, in other words, a basic fear not based upon this experience? What can it be? This can be the fear of the uncertainty, or the fear of the unidentified. For instance, children fear noises, unidentified things. Typically, from the very beginning of human history, people were always terrified of mysterious acts of nature. Or their fear was based on a phenomenon seen before.

For example, fear of the unidentified future, fear of possible fantasized negative events. How do we learn that these are bad events? We compare possible events with skilled negative ones.

It turns out that we fear unknown things because we fear bad unidentified things. We do not fear good unknown things as they make us happy. And when we feel fear, all good events we do forget. Simply put, when we think of an unidentified event in our mind a threatening image appears, as a result, occurs a feeling of fear based upon negative early experienced fear. It means that fear of an unknown thing is a mindful fear.

Chapter 4: Understand The 4 Personality Traits Of The Dark Triad

Narcissism

Someone who is considered a narcissist is likely to have a range of traits that are there. They will have an excessively inflated self-worth, such as seeing that their life is extra special and one of the most important lives in all of history. If this has been inflated enough, they may see that they are the very most important in the whole world.

In the mind of a narcissist, they are not only special, but they are superior to everyone else. They consider themselves to be a better species of a person, higher than what normal people would be. And because a narcissist believes this way, their behaviors are going to change. The behavior that you see in a narcissist is going to reflect the self-worth that the person has.

Some of the outward signs or manifestations of this aspect would include the inability of the person to accept any dissent or criticism of any kind. Even if they feel that someone is trying to criticize them, they are going to have a hard time dealing with this. This kind of person also feels the need to have others agree with them all the time and they like to be flattered. If you are around someone who seems to always have a need for constant praise, recognition, and approval, and if they seem to organize their lives in order to give them constant access to those who will fill this need, then it is likely that you are dealing with someone who is a narcissist.

These three aspects are going to come together to form the Dark Triad. When one person has all of these three traits in them, it can be a hard task to stay away and not get pulled into whatever plan they have. Being on the lookout for these can make a big difference in how much control you have in your own personal life.

We mean a tendency towards grandeur, a continuous search for admiration and approval, a sense of superiority, and a feeling of being special with an effort to accept criticism, which leads to seeking situations and people who give flattery and recognition.

The fantasies of its complete strength and its high feeling of significance are one of the most common features in almost all narcissists. Most of these people are to blame for the continual praise they have received as kids while speaking about these fantasies. As adults, these people will still require love from all over because they have fostered the impression that their colleagues are the most important.

The inflationary sense of self-worth experienced by narcissists internally also has implications for their external reality. This usually shows in two aspects: consent and praise, criticism, or hatred of dismissal. Lobbying and consensus are like oxygen for the narcissistic ego while criticism and dissent are like poison. Picture an inherited dictator to understand how narcissism looks when it comes to its logical conclusion. Such persons ask for the worship of those over whom they have power, the construction of a monument, and complete obedience and appreciation. Any act of disagreement shall soon and brutally be punished. North Korea would be an optimal modern example of the extreme expression of narcissism. The leaders of that nation ask for reverence as Gods and torture anyone who even dares to express an opinion or idea which is not completely in accordance with the official state doctrine.

Machiavellianism

The hallmarks of this trait include a willingness to focus on your self-interest all the time, an understanding of the importance of your image, the perception of appearance, and even the ruthless exercise of power and cruelty rather than using mercy or compassion.

To keep it simple, people who have this trait are ones who always have a strategy when they approach life. The consequences and any ramifications of any action are going to be thought out and then assessed in terms of how they are going to impact the one who is carrying them out. The Machiavellian approach to the world is summed up with a simple question: "How will this action benefit me, and how will my public perception be impacted as a result?"

Machiavellian people are going to be masters of doing what is going to personally serve them well, while still being able to maintain the good public image that they want. This allows the manipulator to do what they want, while still getting people around them to still like them.

It instead indicates manipulative skills, high rationality, and planning to the smallest detail of the moves to the point of justifying even the least adequate means, poor morality, and exploitation of others and situations for one's own advantage.

For many people who do not meet the clinical definition of Machiavellianism, their government figures usually reflect their real private self. Everyone shapes his image and behavior in public a bit, but in general, most people's outward image is nothing more than a polished portrait of who they really are. They often have a good idea of what they are really and the person they often potter in the public eye. Perhaps the finest instance is that of serial killers. Often the best have escaped the grip of the law because their outer picture is the farthest away from their morbid fascination. The most popular instance is that of the famous serial killer, Ted Bundy. According to those who knew him, he was a beautiful guy. He was also very eloquent and just showed that nobody thought that he had a single poor bone in his body. This allowed him to kill up to 30 females before he was finally captured.

Examples of such a difference between the intent and appearance in less extreme fields than serial killing can be discovered.

There are numerous stories of leaders in the company who succeed in ruthlessly cutting employment and making profits as much as possible. With regard to Machiavellianism, the very best of these managers can actually get people to understand that they are compelled or even compassionate! Such rulers are almost role models for those who only want to serve their own wishes and at the same time appear to be 'a person of the people.' Another characteristic of Machiavellian men is the willingness to exploit people. Let us look at an instance to understand this well. A newcomer to a specific office that has such Machiavellian characteristics would see each colleague, boss, or team member as a resource or part of a puzzle to use and use. The Machiavellian would not see other people as fellow humans but would see a series of strategic threats and weaknesses to manage, exploit, or neutralize. This is an important part of why Machiavellians are so aware of how they are. They know that this outward image is the key to efficiently exercise effect and exploit everyone they come across.

Another feature of the Machiavellians is the instillation of fear in their surroundings. This stems directly from 'The Prince,' who urges people to be both fearful and loved at the same time. If this is not possible, the book states that are feared are easier to love. At the same time, the concept of loving and afraid is linked directly to the Machiavellian trait of separating public and private perception. The perfect Machiavellian can inspire fear and obedience in people who genuinely pretend to feel higher love than fear.

Psychopathy

Psychopathy is characterized by the absence of empathy, the scarce presence of remorse, the sense of guilt and anxiety with respect to the consequences of one's sometimes aggressive and unfair action, disinterest in many areas of one's own action, and difficulty in expressing feelings and emotions, resulting in insensitivity.

This is going to refer to a psychological condition that involves a superficial charm, impulsivity, and a lack of commonly held human emotions, such as remorse and empathy. Someone who exhibits enough of these traits can be known as a psychopath. These individuals are seen as some of the most dangerous people because they are able to hide their true intentions, while still causing a lot of trouble.

People often associate the word 'psychopath' with an image of someone who is mad and wields a machete. The reality is different, and this can make it more deadly. A true psychopath is more likely to be that charming and handsome stranger who is able to win over their victim before they ruin those victims' lives in the process.

Interestingly, some of the top people in business score high on psychopathy personality tests. But as time goes on, it is becoming more common to see psychopathy as more of a problem to the victim and to the society rather than an issue in the psychopath's own life. Psychopaths are able to get to the top of anything that they choose because they don't have to worry about some of the compassionate indecisions that other humans are going to experience.

The three characteristic aspects of the dark personality lead to assume significant characteristics in terms of personality and behavior. Specifically, the person with the Dark Triad tends to be manipulative to the point of exploiting the other for his or her own advantage, with a detached and cold attitude towards the consequences generated and a constant thought of grandeur and right, which animates his/her actions.

In the emotional sphere, he seeks strong sensations in different areas, up to performing extreme and dangerous acts for himself or others, without concern, guilt, or moral sense. He has excessive care of himself and his physical appearance, with attention to detail and not caring for external criticisms that are perceived as a manifestation of others' incapacity and ignorance, with consequent closure of relationships animated by these circumstances.

However, they are often attractive and intelligent enough to plan their behavior rationally and punctually.

In all respects, it is essential to understand how this group of people manifest themselves in order to detect them at an early stage and to protect themselves from them. Charm is one of the most common conducts of a psychopath. This charm should be understood to be superficial rather than deep, true charm. If you think of a genuinely charming person from your lifetime, you likely recognize that they have favorable features that support external behavioral displays. However, if a person truly shows a charming person as an expression of goodness, he should not be labeled a psychopath. Psychopaths can demonstrate all external charm signs like physical attraction, apparent warmth, and interest in others. The inner motivation behind these outer flags is why it is so red. As a portion of an equation, psychopaths see the charm. The manipulator often asks him whether it gives the victim a certain emotion to feel in a specific euphoric manner and also whether the outcome is advantageous or beneficial. They are calculative individuals who are addicted to ordinary human emotions. Lying is another feature that really distinguishes psychopaths. All of us lie in our daily life. This doesn't imply we are all psychopaths necessarily. However, when combined with other features it can indicate a psychopathic personality. Lying is as natural for a psychopath as breathing, for most people who are psychologically healthy. A psychopath can present reality convincingly at a certain moment as whatever it needs to be. Furthermore, psychopaths do not show signs of lying outside because they have no emotional attachment or feelings of disgust, guilt, or excitement about their lies. For psychopaths, lying is just 'doing what's needed right now.'

An absence of impulse control is another signature element of psychopathy. Most people have procedures and internal controls that prevent them from acting rapidly. These prevention mechanisms are missing for a psychopath. If a psychopath sees an opportunity to take advantage of it, it is without hesitation or a second thought. This may involve killing someone they want to kill, rape someone, or steal something they want to steal. This cruel impulsiveness is what makes psychopaths some of the most effective people in fields, such as the military and business. The automatic implementation of a crucial action is a characteristic non-psychopaths do not have, and this lack is actually harmful to lives.

The absence of remorse is another feature that distinguishes psychopaths from non-psychopaths. Many people who have committed an atrocity, such as murder, are profoundly guilty of what they have done and taken their own life due to these feelings. Psychopaths don't choose to be remorseful; they can't do it physically. Asking a psychopath to feel remorse is like asking a deaf person to listen to music. The absence of guilt is strongly linked to a lack of remorse. Usually, people feel guilty when they break a certain moral standard, they value themselves. Since psychopaths don't think properly or incorrectly, they just think about what is helpful or unnecessary; their guilt is a foreign concept. The closest to a psychopath's guilt or remorse is regret that he has not conducted his psychopathic deeds in accordance with its own elevated norms.

Sadism

Sadism may not be one of the aspects of the dark triad, but it is still something necessary to add to this. Modern researchers into psychology have proposed that the dark triad is in fact composed of four parts and that a sadistic personality disorder should be added to this. Sadism is sometimes the hardest personality trait to understand here because it is often the least relatable out of all of them.

All of us can point out times in our lives when maybe our personality was a little bit narcissistic, psychopathic, or fit with Machiavellianism. But sadism is a kind of an alien thought, and most people find that this is something that is hard to rationally understand.

Sadism is when the person derives some sort of pleasure from the suffering of others. This could add in a new and worrying dimension to the preexisting traits that we have talked about above. If the Machiavellian leader wanted to cause others to suffer, they would not regret it. But if they were a sadist as well, they would enjoy that suffering. They would actually get some sort of pleasure out of the brutal acts that occur.

The feature that is going to set sadism apart from some of the other aspects of dark psychology is the fact that it is all about cruelty. And this cruelty is just there to provide pleasure for the one using it. It is not there to serve a larger aim. It is not there for some control for the manipulator. Sadists just want to cause the suffering of others because it is entertaining for them and they enjoy watching it, and nothing else.

Often sadism is going to show up with some of the other forms of the dark triad that we discussed above. But it adds in another terrifying part to the mix that it can make it hard for the victim to gain control again. Recognizing the signs early on is one of the best ways to keep yourself safe and to ensure that you are not taken advantage of when someone is using the dark triad against you.

Chapter 5: Identifying Red Flags: Identifying Psychopaths, Sociopaths, Machiavellians, And Narcissists

Even though decades of research have proven that dark psychologists are living among us, they have not yet been categorized as a psychiatric disorder in the Diagnostic and Statistical Manual of Mental Disorders by the American Psychiatric Association. This may be because of the limited amount of research available on dark psychology, especially as it has only been researched in the past few decades. Even the perpetrators of dark psychology have not yet been listed in this book, the research that is available makes it easier to categorize them according to common traits. In the chapter below, you'll learn some of the most common traits of dark psychologists, as well as which of them you should avoid. You will also find a short personality test that can help you determine if you are using dark psychological techniques without realizing it.

Personality Traits of the Average Dark Psychologist

Many people who practice dark psychology techniques believe they are superior to others. Some may even believe that they do not have to follow the same rules as the people around them because they deserve special treatment. Another common trait is a tendency to lie. These types of people lie for the sake of lying, but some may lie and not even realize it.

On the outside, the typical dark psychologist is charismatic and friendly. They have a superficial charm that convinces others to let their guard down, and that is when they weasel their way in. Most of these people also have intense eyes and they may maintain eye contact for a long period of time, to the point where it is uncomfortable. Internally, they are incapable of feeling guilt, shame, or empathy. They either do not want to feel other people's pain or they are incapable of feeling it.

Which Personality Type is the Worst?

According to experts, narcissists are the least threatening of dark psychologists, as they are typically too focused on themselves and their own goals to act maliciously toward other people. Machiavellians typically do not have a moral ground, so they are the next most dangerous of the dark psychologists. While they may manipulate or exploit others to get their way and typically act in an immoral way, they do not generally physically harm or threaten others. Psychopaths and sociopaths are the personality types most likely to cause physical harm. They lack empathy and compassion for others, so they are not affected by anyone else's pain or suffering. They may even be completely emotionally detached for themselves, which makes them incredibly dangerous.

Keep in mind, however, that there are many functioning sociopaths in the world around us. Even though most murderers, rapists, and other hardened criminals are considered psychopaths or sociopaths, they are not always using their manipulative tactics in a way that is meant to cause physical harm. Many of them manipulate people that stand in the way of them achieving their goals or for their own entertainment.

Another type of dangerous dark psychologist is those familiar with neuro-linguistic programming. Someone trained in neuro-linguistic programming can reach the deepest parts of your mind and exercise mind control tactics if you allow them. Check out the next chapter for tips on how to prevent these dangerous personalities from taking advantage of your mind.

How Do I Know if I Am a Dark Psychologist?

Some people have been using manipulation so long they do not even realize there is a problem with their behavior. Others slowly move toward dark psychology. They may be highly in-tune with the emotions and thoughts of others, which lets them use unique intel to get their way. For example, a car salesman might see a woman with slightly messy hair, a coffee stain at the bottom of her shirt, and a keychain with a picture of young children. He can use this information to assume she is a mother, so he might try to sell her a vehicle that is roomy and safe.

Keep in mind that not all persuasion tactics are dark and unethical. To tell the difference between the two, it is important to carefully analyze your intentions. If the intention is only for your benefit, it might be unethical. However, if the outcome is a win-win type of scenario, the manipulation is okay. In the case of the car salesman, there is nothing unethical with selling a mother a roomy, safe car. If he uses her status as a mother to assume she knows nothing about cars and sell her a piece of junk, or overcharge her for a car, that would be unethical because the sale is to benefit him. Here are a few questions you can ask yourself to analyze the persuasion and manipulation tactics you have been using and tell if they are dark or unethical in nature:

• What outcome am I expecting? Who is going to benefit from the encounter and how will they benefit?

• Is my approach honest and open?

• Can I feel confident in my approach? Does it make me feel good inside?

• Is the other person going to experience a long-term benefit because of this interaction?

• Will the strategies I'm using create trust or destroy it?

• Would I be embarrassed or upset if the other person mentioned my persuasion strategies? Could they damage the relationship?

The Dark Triad Test

Research by psychologists Peter Jonason and Gregory Webster narrowed down some of the most common traits shared by the trio of manipulative personalities, including the psychopath, Machiavellian, and narcissist. They developed a test published in 2010, which includes twelve traits considered the 'Dirty Dozen.' By rating someone according to these traits, people can be rated according to which category they fall into and the severity of their behavioral traits. In recent years, this has become a new focus in personality psychology. While you may have trouble scoring someone else, as most dark psychologists are not upfront about their real personality traits, you can use this to evaluate your own personality and if you are prone to using unethical tactics to get your way.

To use this test, read each statement and rate yourself on a score of 1-7, with 1 not applying to yourself and 7 being a strong personality trait.

1. I use manipulation so things go my way.

2. I do not usually have remorse for my actions.

3. I want admiration from others.

4. I do not consider morality before acting.

5. I have lied or used deceit to make something go my way.

6. I can be insensitive and callous.

7. I have flattered others to achieve my goals.

8. Seeking status and prestige is important to me.

9. I am often cynical.

10. I exploit others to achieve my own personal goals.

11. I expect others to do special favors for me.

12. I want others to give me their attention.

A minimum score on this test would be 12, while a maximum score would be 84.

When trying to narrow down personality traits, you can look at the questions. Someone who scored high on statements 1, 5, 7, and 10 is likely to fall into Machiavellianism. Someone who scored high on statements 2, 4, 6, and 9 is likely to fall into psychopathy. Finally, someone who scored high on statements 3, 8, 11, and 12 is likely to fall into narcissism.

One of the first steps in gaining back control of your mental state is learning to identify dark psychologists in your life. While watching out for certain behaviors can help, even these are not always clear as most dark psychologists have a charming personality that they use as a front. In addition to being aware of the dark psychological techniques of others, be aware of the strategies you use to manipulate and persuade. The psychology test provided above can help you decide if you are acting ethically when persuading others or if you need to be more aware of your actions so you can conduct yourself in a more ethical way.

Chapter 6: The Art Of Persuasion

Persuasion is one of the most ancient forms of mental manipulation, and it also applies heavily to dark psychology. Persuasion is a form of verbal manipulation which comes in the form of strong argument or debate and ends with one party changing their course of action to fit with the other party's viewpoint. We see this in everyday life in the course of business dealings and personal relationships. Persuasion doesn't always have to have a negative connotation or a dark psychological impact, but it's a useful tool to learn no matter what your desired outcome or how you choose to use the art of persuasion.

Go Ahead, Twist My Arm

The subtitle above is a phrase often used by people who are teetering towards doing something but just need a final push. Persuading them to do it is often pretty simple. But what about people who are staunch in a belief or course of action?

How can you learn to use your words to have a powerful effect on others?

Think about some of the greatest 'persuaders' in human history. Who comes to mind? Political leaders and religious figures should be on your list. How about inventors and salesmen? People who are skilled in the art of persuasion are those who believe strongly enough in their convictions and have the verbal skills to impart that belief onto others.

Ancient Greek Origins of Persuasion

Persuasion has been taught as a skill and art since the days of the Greek philosophers, who instructed their students in a variety of argument and debate techniques. Aristotle was the foremost of the philosophers to teach the art of persuasion, and he presented three primary areas of focus for learning and using it.

Ethos- Ethos is a method of argument which relies heavily on the character of the speaker. Aristotle taught that in order to make a persuasive argument, the speaker must present themselves as someone who is credible and reliable. This means that in order to argue using ethos, you must choose your language carefully, and mind your appearance. Ethos arguments are well-suited (no pun intended) for business settings.

Speakers who argue using an ethos model are attempting to appear trustworthy and knowledgeable. By seemingly having more authority on a subject than their listeners, the listeners are more likely to be persuaded to come around to the speaker's viewpoint. Trustworthiness can be conveyed through verbal and non-verbal cues, through a well-groomed appearance, and the use of proper language.

This is especially true for sales and business dealings. If you want to use and ethos-modeled argument, make sure you know what the vocabulary and the uniform of that industry. People will be quick to catch on if you call a major supply item or process by the wrong name, or if you show up wearing a wildly inappropriate dress or footwear for a certain task.

Ethos arguments are meant to be authoritative and firm. When delivering one, you must be staunch in your belief, measured in your words, and relevant in your appearance. Mind your body language- it's important to be engaged with your listeners, so make eye contact and use open stances which show that you are not confrontational, just passionate. People are more likely to believe in your argument if they can sense your sincerity. You also want to make sure that you speak in a tone and timber that is strong and varying. Speaking in monotone will lose the attention of your audience.

Pathos- Arguments made on Aristotle's pathos model are arguments that are meant to play directly into the emotions of the listener. The goal of an argument or speech using the pathos model is to elicit emotion, gain the affection of your audience, and use that emotion to bring them around to your way of thinking.

In order to use a pathos-based argument, you must first understand a bit about who you are speaking to. Being able to form a rapport with the audience is key, so if you want to use a pathos model in a formal speech setting, it's important to do a little research about the people you will be interacting with. When using a pathos model argument in a personal setting, it's highly probable that you are already familiar with the emotional state of the person you are trying to persuade.

By finding a correlation between your argument and what your audience (be it one person or one hundred people) already believes, you can find a way to reach what's called their 'anchor'. Anchor points can include personal or religious beliefs, values or morals, or a set of norms specific to your audience. Finding an anchor and using it as a basis for or against your argument means you will have a solid starting point from which to base your case and appeal to their emotions.

The voice you use in a pathos model argument is also very important. Using soft, artful language is more conducive to evoking emotions such as sadness or tenderness, while strong, heavy language will strike up passion or anger. Know your purpose before you choose your words and tone, and you'll be able to craft a more effective pathos-based speech. Remember, the goal of pathos is to create a bond between you and your audience, and language will play a large part in forging that bond and bringing your listeners around to your argument.

Logos- The third style of argument taught by Aristotle is the logos model, which relies on logic and reasoning. This rhetoric can be accomplished in a number of ways, but in modern times, data and hard evidence are more readily available through internet research. This means that logos-based arguments are easier than ever to craft and to back up with sources.

Logos arguments can be extremely useful in business settings, for making sales and closing contracts. Being able to present your case, calmly and firmly with real data and logic, can take you a long way in the business world. Logos arguments are based on structure, evidence, and rhetoric, and those who wish to use this type of argument should be skilled at connecting with people through language and logic.

The goal of a logos argument is to outthink your audience. For every point and counterpoint offered, you should be able to offer another thought to contest the last. By having a strong enough argument to counter all debate, you come out with the strongest rhetoric and your audience almost has no choice but to agree with you. In short, a powerful logos argument should mean that you have the final word.

Standing the Test of Time

Aristotle's three-pronged approach to the art of persuasion has persisted for centuries because the basis of the method is never-changing but adaptable to almost any setting. Aristotle taught that all arguments need three things; a speaker, a subject, and a listener or listeners. These criteria remain the same no matter how much the world around us changes. From Aristotle's open-air schools to internet forums today, arguments are as much a part of human nature as breathing.

If you can parse your argument down to one of Aristotle's rhetorical styles while remembering the three criteria, you can successfully argue just about anything. Taking time to know your audience, research your key points, and being able to relate to others will take you a long way when it comes to the art of persuasion.

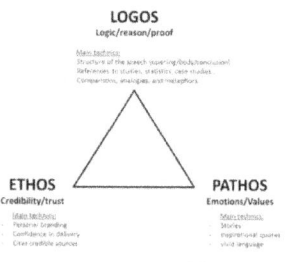

A visual breakdown of Aristotle's 3 models of arguments

Be Stylish

Aristotle also placed a heavy emphasis on the use of style when crafting a successful argument. This didn't mean he asked his students to wear their sharpest togas or finest sandals. When Aristotle talked about style, he meant language and structure that would be conducive to creating the most effective argument for the model you want to use.

For an ethos-based argument, this might mean using more formal and rigid language, to appear professional or authoritative. You want to convince your audience that you know what you're talking about, so you might want to avoid slang or loose language. In a business setting, make sure you are using proper industry terms and lingo.

When using a pathos model, choose a language which correlates with the emotion you are trying to evoke. If you are trying to be sympathetic or garner sympathy, use a softer tone and descriptive words. If you are trying to arouse anger or outrage, short, strong syllables would be more effective. Body language is important here, too. Make sure your verbal and non-verbal cues are conveying the same message.

For logos arguments, clarity is key. Aristotle taught that the facts should not be clouded by the language. Language used in a logos model should be clear, concise, and unclouded by anything that isn't a fact or doesn't have supportable evidence. Arguments in this form should be completely based in logic which cannot be easily refuted.

The way you phrase your words and how you use a tone of voice and body language is crucial no matter which model of argument you choose to use. Poor sentence structure, use of slang, sloppy syntax, and misuse of words can take the best argument and turn it on its head. Be sure to choose your words carefully and put your best mental foot forward.

Practicing Persuasion

Persuasion is a skill which for many people takes time to develop. You can study the speeches of the great persuasive orators. You can write arguments and polish them. You can have mock arguments in your head with yourself. You can practice arguing with strangers on the internet. In all seriousness, though, one of the best ways to improve your language and critical thinking skills is to read. Read things that challenge your way of thinking. Read things that make you think and create counter-arguments. Read things that are translated from other languages and pay attention to the way the words flow.

If you choose to challenge yourself, you'll be much more prepared to take on the challenge of arguing with others, and your chance of winning a persuasive argument will go up exponentially. Remember, the goal is to focus on the outcome you wish to achieve and find a verbal path to that goal.

Using Persuasion in Real Life

Learning about methods of persuasion is one thing, but using those methods in real-life scenarios is the true test of their effectiveness. Think about the ways we see persuasion used daily- let's use the example of a mother cajoling her child into doing something necessary but unwanted, like turning off their morning cartoons to get dressed and go to school. In what way could the mother use the three methods of persuasion to achieve her goal?

Using ethos, the mother could exhibit her authority over her child by telling them that if they don't want to get dressed for school, they will be grounded from the TV for a few days. The mother's willingness to flex that power over her child and her ability to follow through on the threat would persuade her child to do her bidding.

If the mother wants to use a pathos-based argument, she could sympathize with her child. Here, the mother could explain that she understands that it's rainy out and that she doesn't want to get dressed and go to work, but they both need to get started in their day before they get in respective trouble at school and work. Seeing that both mother and child are in the same situation, the child may be more willing to comply with the mother's wishes.

To use a logos argument in this situation, the mother would want to present facts to the child. She could remind them that the bus comes in 15 minutes, and she doesn't have time to drive the child today. If the child doesn't go to school, they'll have too many absences and be suspended or be excluded from a reward-based activity like a school trip or field day.

Which argument the mother decides to use would be based on the personality of her audience- her child. The mother would want to use the most effective form of argument for her child to get them to listen and comply. When using persuasion, be sure to analyze which model will best suit your purposes.

Chapter 7: Different Types Of Dark Psychology And Manipulation Tactics

Dark psychology is all about manipulation. As we have stated in various sections of this book, manipulation is meant to benefit the manipulator. So, when a manipulator sets out to execute one of their schemes, the intent is not to benefit the victim. Hardly. The main intent is to find the means of exploiting the victim in order to achieve the manipulator's objectives.

Often, this requires the use of specific tactics which, when used appropriately, can be very effective in achieving the aims and goals of the manipulator. Now, it should be said that some manipulators are actually quite good at instinctively carrying out these tactics. In other cases, manipulators may be well trained in these types of techniques.

But one thing is for certain: if you want to become good at any of these tactics, you need to practice them regularly. In fact, manipulation is like any other skill. It requires a good deal of practice and experience before you can actually become proficient at it.

With that in mind, we're going to devote this chapter to the discussion of the most effective and thereby powerful manipulation tactics out there. Most importantly, you will be able to recognize them in action, thus giving you the chance to protect yourself against this type of manipulation.

Blackmail

Blackmail is commonly known as having some type of information or knowledge, that if revealed, can be very damaging to the victim. Therefore, the victim doesn't have much choice but to comply with the manipulator. The end result is a negative feedback loop in which the victim has no choice but to go along until they have a chance to escape the trap.

While blackmail is very common as far as holding damning information on someone, emotional blackmail can be just as damaging. This occurs when the manipulator has some type of control over the victim and then uses this control to extort the victim.

Consider this situation:

The manipulator knows that the victim is very insecure about their past. The victim was once an addict and had a stint, or two, in rehab. The manipulator knows that the victim is very concerned about turning over a new leaf and put that past behind them. However, the manipulator threatens to bring up the victim's past every time they want to get something out of them.

Now, you might be thinking, "why doesn't the victim just get away from the manipulator?" That is a fair assessment in the vast majority of cases. However, the manipulator that is able to latch on to their victim does so because the victim is in a vulnerable position.

That is the main takeaway here. When the manipulator is able to recognize that the victim is in a vulnerable position, they are able to use that against them. So, it's important that you recognize if you happen to find yourself in such a position. That way, you can guard against unwelcome attempts.

Coercion

Coercion is the use of any type of resource that forces someone to do something against their will. This may include physical violence, or at the very least, the threat of physical violence. Manipulators generally find out what the victim fears most, and proceeds to attack from that angle. Whenever the victim reveals their fears, the manipulator is able to latch on and take advantage of such a situation.

For example, it's common to see siblings bother each other with items they fear. Let's say that one sibling is afraid of spiders. So, another sibling will use this to get their sibling to do these dishes when it's not their turn.

While this may seem childish, it can be a very powerful tool when used correctly. However, there is a catch to it. The manipulator will have to eventually make good on their threats. Otherwise, the victim will soon realize that the manipulator is just talk and no action. In this case, the jig may be up, and the victim will rid themselves of the manipulator.

Using threats to coerce someone can be useful but bear in mind that they need to be credible threats. At some point, the manipulator will have to show what they are capable of so that the victim remains in a constant state of fear.

Subliminal Messaging

Earlier, we made the point about advertisers seeking to position their brands in the minds of consumers. One of the ways this can be achieved is through subliminal messaging. For starters, overt advertising is the kind that shows a product and a brand attempting to assuage consumers to buy the product. This type of overt advertising can be fun and engaging or downright boring and annoying.

With subliminal messaging, advertisers include a message hidden inside a larger one. These types of messages consist of quick bursts, often lasting less than a second on-screen in which the brand or product is featured.

These messages go unnoticed by the conscious mind because they are so short that the brain doesn't really have a chance to process it. However, the senses do pick it up. The thing is that with the flood of information, the brain may not be able to perceive it.

Think about it this way:

If you drink a gallon of water with a couple of drops of poison, you may not necessarily taste the poison, and while it may be a tiny amount, it's still there. Over time, if you keep drinking drops and drops of poison, they will eventually cause a reaction in you.

The same happens with subliminal messages. These messages are hidden in visual advertising, movies, music and slogans. You may not necessarily perceive it but they're there. A good example of this is a catchy tune. So, the next time you find yourself humming a song that you can't get out of your head, you can be sure that you have just fallen for a subliminal message.

Neurolinguistic Programming

Neurolinguistic programming, or NLP, consists of an audio stimulus being repeated over and over until it is fixated by the subconscious. Going back to music, you often find that there are songs which you hate at first, but since they are played over and over everywhere you go, you end up tolerating them until you find yourself singing along. Such is the effectiveness of NLP.

This is the reason why companies adopt slogans and business coaches have employees use mantras during their working hours. Moreover, mottos and other phrases used to inspire people are means of using NLP to fixate a message in people's minds. Over long-term exposure to such messages, the target audience, at worst, recognizes the message and its meaning. At best, the message is so effective that the target audience is compelled to do what the message says.

A great example of this is the slogan is associated with the world's most successful brands. These slogans automatically tell you what you need to do if you are in the mood for a given product. For instance, soft drink manufacturers spend millions of dollars a year in advertising so that consumers are well aware of what drink options they have whenever they are thirsty.

Another practical application of NLP is positive affirmations. Whenever you hear coaches and gurus tell you to repeat positive affirmations to yourself over and over, you're seeing NLP in action. The reasoning is that after hearing a message (at least in your head) for so long, you'll be prone to internalizing it.

Hypnosis

Hypnosis is commonly used in dark psychology and manipulation but in a very subtle and non-threating manner. When you think about a hypnotherapist telling a patient "you're getting sleepy" while holding a pocket watch, what you're seeing is the hypnotherapist inducing a very calm state in which the target releases their guard. When this occurs, the target's subconscious emerges. At this point, any message can be implanted with very little resistance.

So, how can you achieve a deep state of relaxation in people without using your pocket watch?

A good solution is television. Studies have shown that brainwave activity tends to level off after a little as 30 minutes of watching television. At this point, brainwave activity resembles that of deep sleep. At this point, the individual is literally sleeping with their eyes open. Since brainwave activity has practically ceased, it is easy to implant ideas in the subconscious. Over time, these ideas stick, and you have individuals who are very responsive to your message.

Music is also another form of inducing hypnosis. A catchy tune can level off brainwave activity after a certain amount of time. This enables messages to seep through into the subconscious. You can see this rather overtly in music videos. The tune helps establish the state relaxation while the images get the message across. In the end, viewers get a double whammy of sorts.

Bring It All Together

As you can see, these tactics, on their own, are pretty powerful weapons. They are capable of inducing the type of state which manipulators find especially useful for the purpose of implanting their thoughts and ideas. That is why you need to remain vigilant whenever you see catchy adverts or hear infectious jingles. While this doesn't mean that you should live in a constant state of paranoia, it does mean that you should take what you see in the mainstream media with a grain of salt.

If you are looking to implement these tactics for your personal pursuits, a good rule of thumb is to start off slow and build your way up. For instance, if you're looking to implement NLP in your company, test out a small chant or motto, something like, "today's the best day of my life." At first, your colleagues or employees might think you're crazy. But after a while, you will hear them repeat in their regular conversations. That's how you know your attempts have been successful. Ultimately, you can pick and choose what works best for you. As long as you are aware of what you are doing, you will be able to deal with the outcomes this may produce.

Chapter 8: Powerful Communication Techniques

Communication, quite simply, is defined as the exchanging of information that we do amongst ourselves and other individuals. This exchange of information can take place in the form of speaking, writing, signs, signals or behavior.

If you live in this world, you need to relate to others around you. Nobody can survive without having their needs met, and to have our needs met, whether we like it or not, requires the help of other individuals to do so. And therefore, we need to rely on communication to get by.

Communication is a skill that many don't think twice about, but it is one of the most important skills you could have at your disposal. If you want to know what it is like not to be able to communicate or be understood, just picture a time when you have gone to a foreign country where you do not speak the local language.

Everything suddenly becomes more difficult, doesn't it? You struggle to understand and to make yourself understood, and even simple forms of communication like asking for directions seems like an impossible task. Communication, both verbal and nonverbal, matters. It matters because it helps us relate and collaborate with the people living in the world with us.

There are several reasons why it is important to have effective communication in our everyday life, and those reasons include:

Effective Communication Helps Us Form Relationships

The foundation of all human relationships is how well you can bond with another person. Two people start off as strangers, and how do they form a bond from there? They start communicating. They interact, they start talking and start getting to know one another and slowly, a relationship begins to form, and it begins with being able to communicate effectively with one another.

Effective Communication Helps Express Ideas & Pass Information

Think of all the greatest inventions that we have in our lives today. All of those came to fruition because the inventors were able to communicate their brilliant ideas to the rest of the world. Effective communication is the reason people can facilitate the process of information and knowledge sharing so seamlessly. Without it, a lot of our ideas, thoughts, and points of view would just be trapped inside our head, and we would not know what to do about it. If you can effectively master the art of communication and make it easy for people to understand, your chances of conveying the information without the danger of being completely misinterpreted will increase that much more.

Effective Communication Avoids Misunderstanding

We all know what happens when information is misunderstood or taken out of context. Heated arguments arise, fights happen, and sometimes relationships get severed because misunderstood information causes hurt feelings or hit a sore spot with someone. That is another major reason why effective communication is such a vital skill to possess. You exist in this world; you need to be able to express your messages clearly and to the point to minimize the chances that what you are going to say is going to cause problems for yourself and the people that you are speaking to.

Effective Communication Increases Your Confidence

Have you ever noticed how some of the most successful people in the world seem to ooze confidence? When they speak, the audience hangs onto their every word. That's because they're able to communicate well. When you can communicate effectively, your self-esteem and confidence level rise because you do not doubt at all that you can express and tell people exactly what you want them to know. When you can communicate well, you find that you are no longer shy and awkward when it comes time for you to speak, because you know exactly what to do and how to handle the situation.

Effective Communication Will Help You Go Far

Success cannot be achieved if you are not able to convey yourself properly. When people have a hard time understanding you, how will they be able to get along well with you? If you want to be successful at everything you do in life, you need to confidently be able to communicate effectively, because this is how you are going to set yourself apart from the rest. Do you notice how the most successful people in the world are the ones who can communicate effortlessly?

Mindset for Effective Communication

Before we begin our journey into critical conversations the first thing that we need to look at and master is our mindset. What most people don't know, realize or accept is that our mind is the most underused and most understood organ in the human body. With our minds we can accomplish anything that we can possibly imagine as well as limit ourselves to the most basic of tasks and possibilities.

When it comes to mindset it all comes down to what it is that you want and what you are willing to do or not do to achieve it. When looking at mindset, look at it as a coin. On one side we have everything that we want and desire whereas on the other side of the coin we have all of the excuses and issues that prevent us from achieving our goals. For the majority of us however we walk the edge of the coin looking down at the shiny side of our hopes and desires while favoring or listening to the doubts and echoes from the other side.

This is where the conversation starts. What side of the coin are you going to choose?

Your Self Image

The next layer of our mindset can be found in our self-image. The way that we look at ourselves and the way we perceive others looking at us is a major factor in our mindset and the actions that we engage. For instance, if you are someone who is overweight, doesn't speak well, has a disability or just doesn't feel right physically or emotionally your self-image will be affected by this. One the other side of the coin if you are slender, well educated, has a lot of friends and is healthier than ever your self-image will be greater resulting in more positive outcomes and conversations.

Knowing your abilities and limitations

The third level of mindset is our personal knowledge and understanding of our abilities and limitations. To stat this off I want to first say that no one is perfect. If you believe you are perfect, then you are living in a delusional world and are going to be in for a huge disappointment in life.

However, if you know that you are not perfect and can accept that you have limitations then you have the foundation to build form and grow.

When we know and accept our limitations, we can better position ourselves into situations that we feel comfortable and in control.

If we feel comfortable and in control, we are more likely to be in a better frame of mind to have more intelligent conversations with our inner voices. If, however, we find ourselves in situations that we are not comfortable in it is our job to restructure our mindsets to work in a positive way. And we can do this with critical conversations.

You are an island among many

The final component in regards to mindset is one that is seldom talked about or referred to. This is the knowledge that you are an island among many. What this basically means is that you are responsible for you first and foremost. Where many of us fall into the mindset trap is that we think of others first instead of ourselves. Now, I am not saying that you need to be selfish and self-centered. What I am saying is that at the end of the day when all of the kids are asleep, you are lying there in bed wide awake staring at the ceiling letting the events of the day fill your mind just know that you are one with yourself.

The actions that you perform or fail to perform will ultimately affect you in the end. Your kids will one day go off to school, your spouse may divorce you, you may lose or find another job, get a new house, car or win the lottery or eventually die. It is when we find ourselves in these situations we really begin to have these critical conversations with ourselves. Knowing how we plan to handle these conversations when they arrive will ultimately determine their outcomes.

Developing Assertiveness in Communication

One of the most vital skills to be an effective leader and communicator is developing assertiveness, which is starkly different from aggression. Assertiveness is standing up for yourself and not focusing on pleasing everyone all the time. This is done in a manner that is polite, firm, and non-offensive to others. Assertiveness is taking a balanced, reasonable, and win-win approach that considers the overall good. For instance, "I prefer going to a relaxed coffee shop rather than fine-dine restaurant" is a fairly assertive statement. It doesn't pronounce a judgment about what you want. It gives the other person an opportunity to give his/her view about it too. You are mentioning your preferences in a rational and balanced manner.

Assertiveness is clarifying your needs without using aggression or dominance. While aggressiveness involves disregard for another person's rights or needs, assertiveness is about putting across your needs in a polite, firm, and respectful manner. Unlike aggression that focuses on 'I win-you lose', assertiveness is about win-win. Take the aggressive version of the above-mentioned assertive statement. "We are going nowhere else but a relaxed cafe." This doesn't leave any scope for the other person to offer their views.

Assertive folks may not agree with a person. However, they will still respect the person's right to his opinion, beliefs, ideas, and preferences. They often respect the person's right to disagree. "We can agree to disagree" is a classic assertive statement. You don't give up your stand, and also respect the other person's right to stick to their stand. As an assertive person, you don't allow people to walk over you and know where to draw the line, while also respecting other people's values.

Mutual respect and equality are the buzzwords of assertiveness.

Here are a few strategies to be a more assertive communicator:

One secret tip for building greater assertiveness is practicing in front of a mirror. Pretend that your boss, employee, team member, partner, or friend is standing opposite you. Have a mock interaction with them, where there are getting you to do something you don't to do. How best can you communicate this in an open, polite, firm, genuine, and non-offensive manner? Concentrate on everything from your expressions to words to body language. Watch out for the tone of your voice. How do you emphasize certain words to sound more assertive? When do you pause to create the right effect of what you've just said? Practicing this for a while will help you convey your point in a polite and balanced way.

Use more than "I" statements to accept responsibility for your emotions, thoughts, ideas, and feeling. For instance, instead of "we should never go to that restaurant" say, "I think we should avoid going to that restaurant." It prevents you from appearing dictatorial or dogmatic. Again, if you feel upset about your partner not contributing towards the baby's care, you can say something like, "I feel really upset that I wake up several times in the night. I need your help in caring for the baby."

Always view other people as a force you are working or collaborating with instead of working against.

This is even truer in work settings. Some people are always operating with the mentality that someone has to lose if they have to win. This isn't a sign of assertiveness. In any conflict or tricky communication situation, view people as allies instead of nemesis and try to work out a win-win situation for everyone involved.

Assertive people are seldom ruled by their emotions. Even in the most stressful and tense situation, stay calm and composed. Maintain eye contact with the person and keep your body language relaxed. Keep your tone steady, balanced, and uniform. Your thoughts will automatically mirror your body language. When you keep your tone, posture, and words balanced, the subconscious mind invariably assumes a more confident, self-assured, and assertive stand during disagreements and discussions.

Learn to say no. When you are up for something, learn to say a firm and polite no. There is nothing wrong in turning down things that aren't in line with your own priorities, values, goals, ideals, and preferences. Avoid feeling guilty about refusing other people. Our own negative self-talk induces pangs of guilt within us.

For instance, try reframing your inner voice from "I am not a nice person because I don't loan a part of my salary to a co-worker" with "I deserve to remain financially sound and take measures to prevent risking my financial security."

Another brilliant way to develop a more assertive communication style is putting yourself in the place of a loved one. What if he or she were being put through the situation you find yourself in currently? Would you hesitate to take up for them? It is easier for us to take a stand for our loved ones than ourselves.

Consciously practice expressing your opinion, needs, beliefs, and preferences in an open and clear manner. Don't assume that others will automatically know how you are feeling. This is a major reason for conflicts in relationships. We often assume that people will understand our feelings and needs, and avoid expressing them openly. Being an assertive communicator entails staying genuine, respectful, open, and clear about your needs, opinion, and preferences.

Use the repeated assertion technique for developing greater assertiveness.

It prevents you from being manipulated through verbal traps, misplaced logic, and argument baiting while sticking firmly and politely to your stand. The keywords are "calm repetition."

Stay focused on your point. Let's look at a conversation to understand this more effectively.

"I would love to show you our new range of products."

"No thanks, I am not in the least bit interested in them."

"I also have a fabulous offering running on them for the holiday season."

"That's lovely. However, I am still not interested in seeing them right now."

"Would you like to carry a brochure and think about them?"

"No, I am not interested in them right now. If I decide to purchase in the future, I'll get in touch with you."

You demonstrate a consistent stand throughout the conversation through repetition. Repetition is a powerful form of assertiveness. It tells the other person that you aren't about to budge despite their fancy manipulation and persuasion tactics.

At times, you'll need to use negative assertion in your words to take a more comfortable and balanced look at the negatives in your behavior. This also ends up lowering the critic's hostility. You should embrace your shortcomings and faults with feeling the need to apologize excessively for them. Instead, agree tentatively with the hostile or negative criticism by saying something such as "Yes, you're correct. I don't always actively listen to what you say."

Chapter 9: Step By Step Instructions To Viably Plant A Thought Into The Psyches Of Other Individuals

Finding the connection between the cerebrum and the psyche is one of most prominent difficulties that researchers face in the 21st century. The ramifications of such a disclosure will profoundly change our origination of being a cognizant being, and will effectively affect neuroscience, power, legal law — and brain research. Indeed, even the idea that people demonstration with through and through freedom, a thought that is fundamental to our origination of what our identity is, may turn out be false.

The connection among psyche and cerebrum is presently the subject of incredible discussion. The regular view goes back to seventeenth century French savant René Descartes and his significant work which is regarded as Cartesian Dualism in the real context by him. Descartes isolated the brain from the body with his acclaimed explanation "I think, hence I am," an expression known as "the cogito" after the Latin interpretation "Cogito, thus whole." Descartes established the framework for the manner in which that we generally consider ourselves, today — that our psyche is independent from the matter of our bodies, and it's the wellspring of our sentiments, basic leadership abilities, and the majority of the viewpoints that make us what our identity is. Our psyche, a sort of indefinable "apparition in the machine," gives the requests, and the subservient mind just makes our bodies complete them.

Neuroscientists presently state this isn't — to such an extent that there is no higher-request mind that exists independently from our cerebrum guiding it, no such phantom in the machine. Indeed, the neuroscience position is that there is no psyche by any stretch of the imagination, there is just our mind. Our psyche — our cognizance, our feeling of self — is only a fantasy made by the functions of our cerebrum as it goes through every one of the procedures that we have to it to do to keep us alive. These procedures, did by interfacing the billions of neurons in our cerebrums, incorporate everything from keeping our heart pulsating to, a few neuroscientists state, making moral decisions. Our brains, thus every one of these procedures, have been etched by advancement to empower us to improve decisions that expansion our conceptive achievement.

How could we get to this point? Analyses utilizing fMRI scanners enable neuroscientists to gauge movement in the mind, which associates to contemplations and feelings in human subjects. That in itself just indicates connection, and relationship doesn't preclude a psyche to-cerebrum causal framework. However, progressively increasingly exact mind sweeps have demonstrated that there is action in the applicable piece of the cerebrum before the subject of the investigation is aware of these considerations and feelings. So the idea can't be causing the cerebrum action, on the grounds that the mind action happens before the idea. The possibility that we are willing an activity to occur — that we have cognizant idea — is a fantasy. It was really your mind that caused you to do it.

And when the psyche is a dream, and the majority of our considerations and activities can be decreased to the functions of the mind, does that make brain science excess? In case we're discussing the extremely long haul future, when consistently degree of idea, and each shade of inclination, could be recorded by a mind examine, the appropriate response is possibly. In any case, that situation is far off, and when it occurs by any stretch of the imagination. Furthermore, most experts of neuroscience and brain science imagine that the two controls can exist together, and even supplement one another.

One purpose behind this is brain research and neuroscience have various goals.

Clinicians look to take care of issues by investigating indications, while neuroscientists are looking for the root physical reasons for those side effects. Emotional wellness professionals depend on engaging definitions, in which the indications determine the range or finding. The indications still exist, independent of how they are caused. It's helpful to recall that Freud's very own hypothesis of how the cerebrum functions is false, however realizing that is false doesn't decrease the adequacy of mental methods. "Brain science is required in light of the fact that we can learn valuable, significant things about human instinct without knowing a thing about what goes on in the mind.

In addition, the possibility of a "similarity to mind" is being considered by neuroscientists. A few neuroscientists contend that the cerebrum has a sort of hierarchical level that could demonstration somewhat like a psyche. Understand this isn't a brain as we as a rule portray it. No neuroscientist has confidence in what's known as the "top down" model — that there's a sort of mind-like phantom in the machine that instructs the cerebrum, and the top down model is an abomination to neuroscience. Yet, as per Gazzaniga, the cerebrum's numerous procedures are presently thought to be free, now and then contending, frameworks that are circulated all through the organ. These frameworks may take on an aggregate presence that is created by the mind however is not quite the same as it, a sort of neurological case of the adage "the total is more noteworthy than the parts." (In logical terms, this is known as Emergence.)

It's conceivable that the aggregate framework may take on a portion of the controlling properties that we currently credit to the brain. There is a flat out need for Emergence to jump out at control this abounding, fuming framework that is going on at another level. This thought, in any case, is disputable among neuroscientists, and may considerably verge on logical blasphemy.

The science appears to be sound, however many are wary of the possibility that our awareness is a result of our cerebrum forms. At a principal level, there is no logical concurrence on what it really intends to be cognizant — the state has no widespread logical definition. Cynics call attention to that it's nonsensical to ascribe cognizance to the mind and when we don't have a clue what awareness really is. In any case, neuroscientists react this is only the point — it's neuroscience that holds the way in to a meaning of awareness, and the riddle of its reality will at long last be understood by their order.

However, neuroscience would not get much of anywhere without brain science to direct it, writing in Cognitive Daily: Psychologists have distinguished numerous wonders for which neuroscientists presently can't seem to discover similar to movement in the cerebrum. Neuroscientists can utilize research like this to direct their work... Together, brain science and neuroscience can help every one of us see how the cerebrum shapes conduct.

Roisner feels that the future will see neuroscience and brain research meeting up to discover new medications for psychological instability. "In the momentary the most significant impact [of neuroscience research] will be to urge us to change the manner in which we consider manifestations, concentrating on proximal causes at the degree of the cerebrum and how these identify with mental procedures. Longer term, the expectation is that by perceiving unthinking heterogeneity we will grow better order frameworks, new ways to deal with intercession, and further apparatuses to empower specialists to pick the correct treatment for the perfect person.

With karma, and a great deal of logical research, we'll be capable not simply to analyze psychological maladjustment from outside the black box of the mind, however fix it by peering inside. Brain research and the human personality are inseparably connected. Surely, the word brain research is gotten from the Greek words psyche, which means brain or soul, from which the term mind emerged; and logos significance study or talk.

Consolidating these words gives you an exacting interpretation of brain research as being investigation of the psyche. It is obvious, in this way, to discover the idea of the brain at the core of numerous meanings of brain science e.g, "Brain science is the logical investigation of individuals, the brain and conduct." (The British Psychological Society).

When you know a significant objective that another person has, and when you can orchestrate circumstances with the goal that they just accomplish their objective by acting in specific ways, at that point you can control their conduct for whatever length of time that they keep on pursuing that objective.

This essential rule is the premise of things like commendation, support, and discipline. And when you need acclaim from somebody, they will have the option to get you to act in different ways by applauding you when you do. Stickers work in schools since we first instruct kids that stickers are incredible things to have, and after that, when we have them needing the stickers, we possibly give the stickers to them when they do what we require.

In any case, this delicate relationship of controlling conditions to see individuals act in specific ways depends completely on those individuals' objectives. At the point when stickers don't "work" anything else, as in other individuals won't do what you need them to do to get your "stickers," every one of that has happened is that those individuals have changed their objectives about needing stickers. Maybe, presently, the objective to wrap you up is more alluring than the objective to collect stickers.

What is regularly overlooked with a sticks-and-carrots ethos is that in the case of something is a stick or a carrot is resolved totally by the individual to whom the stick or carrot is being applied. A "carrot" is just something an individual needs and a "stick" is something the individual needs to keep away from.

What individuals need can change; when this occurs, the scene of sticks and carrots changes, as well. Nourishment can frequently be utilized to get eager individuals to carry on specifically ways; and when somebody is on a craving strike, notwithstanding, sustenance will be a pointless controller. A few people will do a great deal of things for cash yet not in any case that takes a shot at everybody. Toward the day's end, it's everything relative.

At whatever point you're feeling just as someone else is by all accounts testing your good humor or controlling you here and there, you may be totally right. In any case, rather than requesting that they change what they're doing (which could likewise be a valuable technique) it might be useful to check your very own objectives: What's critical to you right now? What do you need? What objectives are at the front of your psyche? And when you can some way or another change your own objectives you will likewise change the elements of the association with the other individual. Changing your very own objectives isn't in every case simple however it tends to be significantly simpler than changing someone else.

Because of the manner in which we are structured, other individuals can control our conduct. It's likewise a reality, however, that they just control our conduct by controlling the degree to which we can accomplish objectives that are essential to us. It's our very own private gathering of objectives that figures out what will be sticks and carrots for every one of us. By becoming acquainted with our own objectives better we will have the most obvious opportunity with regards to creating fulfilling connections and producing the existence we need.

What is Psychology?

Brain research: the study of the psyche

Human conduct: the crude information of brain research

Brain research and different orders

Parts of brain science

Brain science: the study of the psyche

Brain science is the study of the psyche. The human personality is the most mind boggling machine on Earth. It is the wellspring of all idea and conduct.

How do therapists study the brain?

In any case, how might we study something as perplexing and puzzling as the brain? Regardless of whether we were to part open the skull of a ready volunteer and examine, we would just observe the gloopy dim matter of the mind. We can't see somebody thinking. Nor would we be able to watch their feelings, or recollections, or recognitions and dreams. So how do therapists approach concentrating the psyche?

Truth be told, therapists receive a comparable way to deal with researchers in different fields. Atomic physicists intrigued by the structure of molecules can't watch protons, electrons and neutrons legitimately. Rather, they anticipate how these components ought to carry on and devise analyses to affirm or discredit their desires.

Human conduct: the crude information of brain research

Along these lines, clinicians utilize human conduct as a hint to the functions of the brain. Despite the fact that we can't watch the psyche straightforwardly, all that we do, think, feel and state is dictated by the working of the brain. So clinicians accept human conduct as the crude information for testing their speculations about how the mind functions.

Since the German clinician Wilhelm Wundt (1832-1920) opened the main exploratory brain research lab in Leipzig in 1879, we have taken in a colossal sum about the connection between cerebrum, psyche and conduct.

Brain science and different orders

Brain science lies at the crossing point of numerous other various orders, including science, medication, semantics, theory, human studies, humanism, and computerized reasoning (AI).

For instance, neuropsychology is aligned with science, since the point is to delineate regions of the mind and clarify how each supports distinctive cerebrum capacities like memory or language. Different parts of brain research are all the more firmly associated with drug. Wellbeing therapists help individuals oversee malady and agony. Thus, clinical clinicians help ease the enduring brought about by mental issue.

Parts of brain research

Any endeavor to clarify why people think and carry on in the manner that they do will unavoidably be connected to some part of brain research. The various controls of brain science are amazingly wide-extending. They include:

Clinical brain science

Intellectual brain science: memory

Intellectual brain science: knowledge

Formative brain science

Transformative brain science

Scientific brain science

Wellbeing brain science

Neuropsychology

Word related brain science

Social brain science

You can become familiar with these controls by choosing from the rundown of connections on the correct hand side of the page.

What all these various ways to deal with brain research share for all intents and purpose is a longing to clarify the conduct of people dependent on the operations of the psyche. What's more, in each territory, clinicians apply logical strategy. They define speculations, test theories through perception and try, and examine the discoveries with measurable systems that help them recognize significant discoveries.

Step by step instructions to control individuals' psyche

Would someone be able to control individuals' psyches?

While this may seem like a detestable inquiry you will get astounded to realize that specific types of mind control occur on practically consistent schedule.

When you attempt persuade somebody to have confidence in something you are really controlling his brain, when you attempt to dazzle somebody you are really controlling his psyche and when you attempt to find a new line of work you will really be controlling the psyche of the questioner.

So after all mind control can be something worth being thankful for whatever length of time that you don't utilize it in a non-moral manner. In this article I will disclose to you how you can control individuals' mind's.

Understanding individuals' brains

Straightforward proposals can control minds and can even transform into strong convictions that dwell inside those psyches. The main thing that can keep a proposal from transforming into a conviction is the nearness of a restricting conviction, in any case, and when no repudiating convictions were discovered, at that point recommendations can without much of a stretch control individuals' psyches.

Here is a straightforward model, and when you acted such that caused you to seem like a notable individual numerous individuals will really begin to accept that you are significant and commendable!

That is the reason acting certain is probably the most ideal approaches to control individuals' psyches.

Concentrates found that fake treatments can now and then have a similar impact as genuine prescriptions, this stands valid for discouragement meds!

Again proposals in such case, which originated from a position figure, controlled individuals' brains and changed their perspective.

Numerous individuals reveal to me that they need others to regard them and accept that they are commendable yet just a couple of them understand the way that whatever they propose to individuals can change their convictions.

Walk like a notable individual, talk like a notable individual, manage individuals while placing a similar idea at the topmost region of the listing, and in the blink of an eye you will understand that individuals think the equivalent of you!

Devices for mind control

So what are the devices that you can use to control individuals' psyches?

1) Direct proposals: Talking to individuals straightforwardly can control their psyches as it were. Anyway a few people can channel your words in light of accepting that you have a shrouded inner plan. For instance an individual may feel that you need to show individuals that you are the best just to dazzle them.

2) Actions: Actions are substantially more successful than words as a primary concern control. The most ideal approach to intrigue individuals is to not discuss yourself yet to rather demonstrate to them that you can do amazing things. Indeed, even an extremely basic activity, for example, chatting with certainty can enable you to control individuals' brains

3) Using others: One of the most ideal approaches to send recommendations to individuals' brains is to utilize normal companions. And when somebody rehashed your equivalent proposal, ideally in your nonappearance, at that point it will be bound to stick in the psyche of the individual who heard it. For instance, and when you figured out how to give a typical companion a chance to discuss how extraordinary you are in your nonappearance then this recommendation will probably turn into a strong confidence in the psyche of the individual who heard it

Chapter 10: Dark Manipulation Techniques

Dark seduction is about and why someone may choose to use this kind of seduction to get what they want out of a relationship. The guiding principles that come behind these approaches to seduction, it is time to learn some of the techniques that the dark seducer can use to make dark seduction work for them.

The first approach that we will look at is known as the indirect approach. One mistake that you may see in conventional dating is that one or both parties will offer an icebreaker, one that is usually unappealing and cheesy, when they try to introduce themselves to someone new. They may say something like "You look pretty," "Nice eyes," or "Good song, right?"

Why are these icebreakers so bad? It is likely that the victim of your seduction has heard these countless times, and as soon as they hear them, they will be turned off and not want to talk to you at all. When the seducer uses such a bad line, it often leaves the impression that they are unappealing and bland, and no one wants to waste their time on a relationship with that kind of person.

With the indirect opener, the seducer is throwing in a breath of fresh air compared to the opening lines we talked about before. An indirect opener is going to be an icebreaker that will start the social interaction but won't convey any sexual intent. Often it is going to be posed as an "intriguing question." A good example of this would be when the seducer asks something like "Settle this for me or my buddies over there – do men or women lie more?" This is a different way to open up and talk with the other person and can start up a new conversation. And it shows the victim that the seducer is very interesting and is interested in a good conversation.

These indirect openers have the advantage of eliminating the possibility of rejection. The person who uses this kind of opener is not really offering themselves to the victim of the seduction. It is basically impossible to reject something that wasn't even offered, so it takes that part out of the equation.

Examples Techniques

Another technique to use with dark seduction is social proof. People who are popular are going to be more attractive compared to those who aren't. It is a human instinct to assume that if another person is liked by a lot of people, then there must be something that makes that person likable.

Social proof is an example of showing is more powerful than telling. Many people will try to talk about their success or their popularity, but this isn't a good idea. It is going to seem like you are bragging and can be a big turnoff to the other person. It is better to simply make sure that you are at a table or near others who are interesting. This is going to convey your social value, without seeming like you are showing off in the process.

Of course, social proof can be used for devious purposes. Think about a psychological seducer who is at a club or a bar. They see a girl that they want to seduce. Rather than directly approaching this person, they will decide to approach someone else and start a conversation with them, before moving over to their original target. This can remove the idea that the seducer is lonely, and it can sometimes spark a little jealousy that works in advantage to the seducer.

You can also work with a frame of leading to help with dark seduction. Many times you will find that the people you meet are happy to be led. Indecisiveness is one of the least attractive qualities in others. If you are able to show that you are decisive, you can automatically get the attention of others.

There are several ways that the dark seducer can show their decisiveness and that they have the ability to lead. Some of these could be physically moving around a venue, making the suggestion that it is time to change venues and not being scared to disagree with what someone else has said. Many men try to be indecisive around their victim because they don't' want to come off as weak. This is going to work against them. A dark seducer knows that they need to be decisive if they want to have any chance with the other person.

In addition to some of the techniques that we have talked about above, there are some seducers who are able to harness some of the other dark psychology traits, such as the use of psychopathy, in order to reach their romantic goals. For example, one trademark of psychopathy is the ability of the seducer not to feel any fear when they interact with other people.

Many times a man or a woman is going to be paralyzed by fear, especially when there is a chance for rejection by someone they are interested in. A dark seducer is not going to have this fear because they just don't understand the fear at all. Even if you are not a dark manipulator and you don't regularly use dark seduction, you can use this idea. A psychological seducer is going to learn, over time, that it is better to be the one who tried and failed rather than the one who didn't have any confidence to try in the first place.

Why Are Dark Seducers So Dangerous?

A dark seducer can be a formidable foe. They know exactly how to get the other person, their victim, to fall in love with them. But the problem comes with the fact that the dark seducer really isn't in love with the other person. There is something that the dark seducer wants out of the relationship. This could be companionship because they don't like to be alone, sex, or something else. But they are usually not looking for love at all.

As soon as the victim of this seduction doesn't provide the thing that their seducer wants, the seducer is going to leave. So, if the victim starts to feel that they are being used and withholds sex from the seducer, the seducer will simply leave the relationship and move on to their next victim.

The seducer has no worries about the other partner in the relationship. A true seducer is only going to see the other person as a tool, something that helps the seducer get the pleasure that they want. As soon as that tool stops doing the job that it's supposed to, the seducer will move on to find a new person to do the work for them.

A dark seducer may move quickly between one relationships to the next, or they may even stay in a relationship for a long time. It all depends on the situation and how long the seducer is able to keep the victim under their control. Some victims stand up for themselves pretty quickly. The longer the victim is under the control of the dark seducer, the harder it is for them to leave.

This doesn't mean that the dark seducer has learned how to love their victim. It simply means that the dark seducer has become used to the way that things are, and they will use their powers and their mind control techniques in order to keep the victim right where they are.

How to Avoid Dark Seduction

While some men may choose to use some of the ideas of dark seduction in order to help them gain some confidence, avoid some issues with their fear of rejection, and make it easier for them to meet women, there are many that will use these techniques because they don't really care about the other person at all.

If you do end up getting into one of these relationships, it can be devastating. The dark manipulator is really skilled at using the dark seduction techniques to get what they want. They will find a victim who is vulnerable, and they will present the right solution that the victim needs at that time. For example, they may find a victim who just got out of a major relationship, and they will step in to feel the need of that victim to not be lonely any longer.

The seducer is going to be charming, fun, and the perfect person for that victim. The victim may feel like they have found their soulmate, but the seducer is just there to get what they want out of the relationship. Sure, it may last for some time, but as soon as the victim is no longer meeting the needs of the seducer, the seducer will be gone.

This will leave the victim hurt and broken. They may have overly trusted the seducer (because the seducer is skilled at reading the victim and knew exactly what to do and say to gain that trust and get what they want), and now they are broken. They may go through depression and anxiety and even have trouble trusting others in the future.

Because of all these negatives that come with dark seduction, it is important to watch out for the signs. If you run into dark seduction with a narcissist or with a psychopath, it is even more important to watch for the signs. These individuals are not there to care about what the other person wants. They simply look out for themselves, they feel that they deserve what they want, and they don't have the capacity to care about how it is going to harm the other person.

Due to the way that the relationship was started, including the romance, attraction, the mutual feeling that you found a soulmate (all created by the seducer to get what they want), when things start to take a lot of wrong turns, it is likely to be too late for you, the victim, to walk away. This can be especially true if you went into that particular picture without a good idea of what you wanted in the relationship. Without this clear picture, you would not have the determination to walk away from that relationship when it didn't meet your expectations.

This is why you must always make sure that you know what you want to get out of the relationship before one begins. This will help you be prepared if the relationship becomes something else because you will be able to see when it is going away from your chosen course. You will give yourself a chance to see it for what it is before you damage your self-worth so much where you will stay in that relationship and accept the bad treatment.

This can be hard. Many times we feel that we need a relationship like we are not worth anything unless we are in a relationship with someone else. Then, when we are not in a relationship, we are going to feel like something is missing, and we jump into the first relationship that comes available. This is where the issues will start.

Before you jump into the next relationship, it is important to take some time to soul search. Remember that there is nothing wrong with not being in a relationship all the time.

The first thing that you should do here is to start with some deep thinking and even some soul-searching and decide on the details of the relationship that you are looking to enjoy at that time in your life. Describe what you want out of the other person in this partnership. Describe how you want to feel in this relationship. Set out some clear boundaries and then make sure that you understand why you have these boundaries.

Chapter 11: Myths And Misconceptions About Dark Psychology

There are a variety of subjects that are appropriate for dinner discussion. Dark Psychology is not one of them. The last thing you want to know at Thanksgiving is how Uncle Joe performed on his Machiavellian orientation. Due to the maliciousness around Dark Psychology, there are generally very few accessible conversations on the subject.

Take the Dark Triad experiment, for example. Are you thinking of taking it? If so, are you willing to disclose your findings with anyone? The strong odds are that if you responded positively to the first query, you would presumably respond negatively to the second question. Many people want to speak of themselves as decent citizens.

Furthermore, they want other people to think of them as nice individuals. Putting your Dark Triad evaluation on show for everyone to see might not help this objective. Because of all this hush-hush around Dark Psychology there are, however, several assumptions and misconceptions concerning character traits that are critical to Dark Psychology. This chapter discusses these myths and misconceptions, thus throwing some light onto them.

MYTH ONE: Psychopaths and sociopaths are the exact same thing.

TRUTH: Psychopathy and sociopathy are two distinct forms of antisocial personality conditions.

The words "psychopath" and "sociopath" are used synonymously in daily conversation. However, the two characteristics are very distinct from each other and there are some differences between these two personality disorders. Experts find sociopathy to be a less severe condition than psychopathy. The list below illustrates some of the features that differentiate a psychopath from a sociopath.

PSYCHOPATH:

I. Lacks moral scruples.

II. They are willing to fit in by being attractive and are therefore more difficult to spot.

III. Cold-hearted and highly tactical.

SOCIOPATH:

I. Has a poor conscience.

II. Don't have any intention of fitting in and are therefore easy to identify. Will only be concerned about themselves in the first place.

III. Hot-headed, trying to jump without checking.

MYTH TWO: Psychopaths are born and are not raised.

TRUTH: Psychopaths are indeed born that way.

Psychopathy is a very complex personality disorder that more often than not begins at birth. Psychopaths emerge out of the womb already programmed to behave differently from most people. As a consequence, they move away from what is normal and often find themselves in situations in which any other "average" individual would not typically find themselves. A study has shown that the psychopath's brain functions in a different manner relative to the brains of other individuals who do not have any personality disorders. So what happens when a psychopath is born?

Depending on the type of setting in which the psychopath emerges, they will grow into one of the following pathways. If a toddler who exhibits indications of psychopathy grows up in a supportive family, he or she would be expected to become a corporate or political figure with a lot of power. If the infant grows up in a dysfunctional or abusive setting, he or she is likely to become a serial killer or murderer. Psychopaths who are molded in an atmosphere that is somewhere between the first two conditions end up in positions of control in areas such as law enforcement and administration.

MYTH THREE: Sociopaths are born that way.

TRUTH: Sociopaths are primarily the result of their surroundings.

More often than not, sociopaths are the product of the society in which they are raised. It often begins with a biological or hereditary propensity to sociopathy, which is then compounded by the form of care they receive. For example, a boy who grows up in a society where nobody appears to care for him is likely to have the same lack of sympathy for others in his later life. When children grow up around parents who possess little sense of morality and have no social code, their morals will be profoundly weakened as a result.

MYTH FOUR: Women cannot be psychopaths.

TRUTH: There are reported cases of female psychopaths.

More often than not, when you hear the word "psychopath" you immediately assume it is a male character. Furthermore, Hollywood has done its best to show psychopaths as ax-wielding males on a rampage for murder. It is crucial to recognize though that psychopaths can also be female. Nevertheless, unlike their male peers, female psychopaths are less prone to be physically offensive or abusive. Instead they utilize their sexuality and womanhood to exploit others. Female psychopaths also tend to have a large number of intimate partners.

MYTH FIVE: Psychopaths are fascinated with murder.

TRUTH: Psychopaths are enthusiasts.

Murder is just one of the ways that psychopaths quench their need for exhilaration. When most people think about psychopaths, they think of the massacres that happen left, right and center. Though while it is possible that a murderer is more likely than not to be a psychopath, it is also clear that some psychopaths are no more likely than the majority of the citizenry to commit murder. Most psychopaths go through their life in pursuit of thrills but never really cause violent damage to anyone. Yes, they could break a few hearts when they hop from one romantic partner to another and throw a few people under the bus to scale the professional ladder, but that is as far as many of them go. If you are searching for a psychopath in your life, you are unlikely to find one if you are only searching for brutality and lust for blood.

MYTH SIX: Psychopathy is a mental disorder that can be treated.

TRUTH: Psychopathy is a personality disorder that has no treatment.

If it were a mental disorder, there would be a chance of therapy. Psychopathy, however, is a personality disorder, and this means that there is no treatment that would make psychopaths calm, emotional and empathetic. Because they don't accept that something is wrong with them either, they would not even be concerned about medication, even if it did exist. In situations where psychopaths have been persuaded to try therapy with the intention of fixing broken relationships, it is not unusual to find them trying to manipulate the other party into believing that the therapy is effective or has already worked. Note that these people are extremely deceptive and capable of using whatever methods are necessary to overcome challenging circumstances. Owing to their brazen lack of fear and compassion, a psychopath will have no trouble wasting a loved one's time in therapy, if only to make it seem like they are trying.

MYTH SEVEN: You can transform an individual on the Dark Triad by treating them appropriately.

TRUTH: Most of the individuals who rank highly on the Dark Triad evaluation continue so for the remainder of their lives.

Love is a curious phenomenon in that it lets people feel that they are capable of the impossible, even though the truth is revealed before their eyes. If you are in a relationship with an individual who scores high on a Dark Triad check, the first few weeks of your engagement are likely to be joyous. Manipulative characters have a way of love-bombing you into assuming that they are the perfect match that you have been looking for all along. Sadly, this is typically just an effort to draw you into a friendship that is simply smoke and mirrors. When someone has gotten into this kind of partnership, and the true character of the manipulator then surfaces, in many cases you will see a romantic partner hanging around with the belief that things will improve and love will be sufficient to turn things around. Unfortunately, this is mostly never the case.

First of all, the fact that psychopathy is mostly inherited indicates that it is impossible to overcome it. At best, psychopaths can only turn their lack of empathy into goals that are not harmful to social structure as a whole. As for Machiavellianism and narcissism, these often derive from profound psychological distress that may take a great deal of strategy to conquer. Most people are going to lean heavily towards Machiavellianism and narcissism as a defensive mechanism. Every effort to get them out of this state will only appear to them as an assault, leading them to mount their resistance. As such, interference in the form of love can be extremely inefficient. It is also important to remember that love and other shimmering feelings are not necessarily highly rated by a person in the Dark Triad. They may not even recognize love regardless of how it seems. As such, if you are in a relationship with a partner who has the traits of the Dark Triad, you might want to reconsider whether that is what you desire.

MYTH EIGHT: Individuals who rank high on the Dark Triad are more alluring.

TRUTH: This has been proven to be false.

Why is it that people still tend to be drawn towards the narcissists and the psychopaths of this world? Is it because the Dark Triad characters are more appealing than most of us? In an attempt to ascertain if Dark Triad characters are better-looking, academic scholars have investigated a variety of individuals with higher Dark Triad ratings. The findings of this research indicated that the main reason why these participants looked appealing was that they dressed and portrayed themselves physically in a way that was well organized. When they were clothed in bland clothing, these individuals didn't seem as appealing as before. As such, it is almost reasonable to believe that the care and energy that goes into getting dressed and the confidence that comes with it are what renders a narcissist or psychopath more appealing than they are.

MYTH NINE: Psychopaths can improve when they have children.

TRUTH: Psychopaths are unable to be empathic or responsible for their offspring.

Psychopaths typically have a very difficult time raising their children. Unlike average parents who are not on the Dark Triad scale, it is challenging for psychopaths to view their children as different individuals. Rather, they perceive them to be devices or extensions of themselves that are accessible for their use whenever they wish. Psychopaths are more inclined to see their children as achievements that make them feel good than as young, emotionally fragile beings who are looking for somebody to protect them throughout their early lives. As such, a psychopath will usually force their children to develop skills in something they have no desire to participate in, even though it may be to the detriment of the children's mental health and development. They could forcefully sign them up for swimming classes, for example, as they feel that their child will become an excellent swimmer and a champion, just to boost their social status in the neighborhood. It is very difficult to convince psychopathic parents to see that they are used to excelling only themselves and they will not comprehend why their children will not do whatever it takes to get to the highest level.

MYTH TEN: You are either on the Dark Triad, or you are not.

TRUTH: The Dark Triad is a scale on which some feature highly while others appear further down.

The characteristics of narcissism, psychopathy and Machiavellianism are rooted in every individual. The only distinction is that in some individuals, these behaviors are amplified to the extent that they often become toxic to those around them. Take narcissism, for example. Everyone has their own way of thinking about themselves. You are more likely than not to choose to have decent thoughts about yourself. You like to think that you are nice-looking, intelligent and easy to love. For a narcissist, this self-image is taken out of context to the point that their entire life circles around it. It is not sufficient for them to believe these thoughts about themselves; they also want everybody else to acknowledge that they are great and sacred and that everything about them is brilliant.

Psychopathy is a continuum too. Everyone has a position on this continuum. Think of it this way: have you ever done something that wasn't so good, but you didn't feel bad about it? Have you ever behaved in such a way as to indicate that you are not sympathetic towards someone? If you have replied yes to any of these queries, then at least once in your life, you have displayed psychopathic tendencies. This doesn't mean that you are going to kill someone later in your lifetime. It only means that there are occasions where you will have the psychopath in you come out and other times where you might just be able to keep yourself in check. Catch yourself just in time. The way you have been raised has an impact on whether you are in a position to prevent yourself from releasing your innate psychopathy.

MYTH ELEVEN: Your boss is psychopathic.

TRUTH: Your boss may or may not be a psychopath.

It is the case that many psychopaths who do not become hardened criminals tend to be extremely influential in business, politics and other sectors. Nonetheless, this is not a sufficient excuse to suspect your employer of being a psychopath. Some people are simply motivated and persistent, because what they know and believe is a prerequisite for achievement.

In either case, not a lot of people have sleepovers and happy hours with their bosses. A certain structure is expected from the manager-employee interaction. Your persistent ruthless manager may be a different character when they are not wearing their "boss hat." Do not assume that everybody in a position of power is a sociopath or a psychopath. It doesn't always work like that.

MYTH TWELVE: Your ex-partner is a psychopath.

TRUTH: The relationship may have culminated on a bad note. This does not make either of you psychopathic.

A large number of people like to refer to an ex-partner as a "psycho." Occasionally, a relationship ends on a happy note, where both partners will tend to be best lifelong friends. Regrettably, this is not how most relationships turn out. Most courtships conclude in anguish, allegations and name-calling. Before you call your ex-partner a psychopath, analyze the characteristics in this chapter and figure out if your ex's actions suit any of these. Of course, this doesn't matter if you are through with the relationship, but it might prevent you from getting to fall into the same trap of meeting someone who has the same indications. If you are presently working with someone who displays any of the signs listed here, you might want to contemplate quitting for your sanity. It is necessary to understand that the act of leaving a psychopath or narcissist is distinctive from that of leaving a sane person who does not view the resignation as an insult to themselves. There is a range of resources open to those trying to escape dysfunctional and coercive relationships. Such tools can be accessed in a quick online search.

Chapter 12: How To Use Dark Psychology And Manipulation In Daily Life

People use psychology within their daily lives, so why not use Dark Psychology and the tactics to protect yourself in everyday life. There are quite a few personality traits that can be very harmful if you get caught up in them. Sadists fall under this category. For instance, this personality type enjoys inflicting suffering on others, especially those who are innocent. They will even do this at the risk of costing them something. Those diagnosed as sadists feel that cruelty is a type of pleasure that is exciting and can even be sexually stimulating.

We do have to face the fact that we manipulate people and deceive people all the time. When it comes to deception, people are deceiving others daily, but they are also deceiving themselves. People often lie to gain something or to avoid something. They might not want to be punished for action, or they might want to reach a goal, and they self-deceive to get there.

Here are some examples of how people can deceive themselves:

Having a hard time studying - this is a common occurrence. When people are trying to learn, they find many things that can distract them, especially cell phones and social media apps. They will find just about anything to distract them from the task at hand. These types of people seem to have a phobia of not studying long or well enough, and they are afraid that they will come home with a bad grade, and it will show how unintelligent they are. So, they take the art of self-deception and develop the idea to help prevent them from studying. This excuse will weigh better in their mind if they do end up getting a bad grade on their test. The person's subconscious tells them that it is better for them to get alarming rates for lack of studying than to study and to fail and therefore having to blame their intelligence. They couldn't live with that.

Here are other ways that we regularly deceive ourselves:

Procrastinating – People often waste time when they do not want to study or do something meaningful. However, the main reason for procreating could be the phobia against failing, and procrastinating was just an excuse. Self-confidence can be an issue as well.

Drinking, doing drugs, and carrying out bad habits -People often fall into bad habits, consume, or do drugs just to have something to blame if they lose again. This type of person will try to convince themselves that if they could stop doing drugs, they could be very successful when they deceive themselves and stand in their way.

People often hold back because life is unfair. They tell themselves that we all live in a big lie that most people believe in, but not them. It is easier to blame it on life being unfair then hold ourselves accountable for not reaching our goals.

If you realize that you have been deceiving yourself, here is a couple of things that you can do to change that.

Remember that you are smart, and the fact that you have been able to deceive yourself reaffirms it. If you were not wise, there would have been no way that you would have been able to come up with some of those ideas.

It is essential to learn how to face your fears. If you are running from a specific trauma or not wanting to take a test, you have to remind yourself that you are stronger than this and that you can beat it.

Lastly, once you face your fears, your self-confidence and courage will grow.

Chapter 13: The Techniques Used In Dark Persuasion

There are many different types of techniques besides the ones we talked about earlier, which you can use when it comes to dark persuasion. These will ensure that you can get what you want from the other person and that someone can take advantage of you. Some of the different dark persuasion techniques you can use for your benefit will include:

Love Bombing

Another persuasion technique you can work with will be known as love bombing. The idea that arises from the attacks of love is not new. It was first used in the 70s by Sun Myung Mood, who was the head of the United Unification Church. It was used in a way to describe the kind of happiness and love that his followers would show others to convince them to join the church. According to Psychology Today, this method has also been used by many other groups, including gang leaders and protectors, to achieve the obedience and loyalty they desire.

In recent decades, however, many psychologists will use this term to talk about some of the disturbing behaviors they will see in some of the romantic relationships out there. This type of love bombing will be a kind of seductive tactic designed to ingratiate and create positive feelings in the other person. Many tactics can be used with this, including praise, gifts, flattery, attention, and a lot of affection.

Excessive is one of the keywords we need to consider when it comes to this tactic. The bombing of love will be different than some of the behaviors that are seen as usual in a relationship, and sometimes it will seem unwarranted or inexorable. And sometimes, depending on how the receiving partner decides to draw attention, it would seem that it is too good to be true.

Just like what we can imagine in war, the love bombings will be like a big assault on the gates in the hope of breaking down any resistance. Each of us will have a wall that we put around ourselves to make sure we won't be damaged. The person who becomes the victim of this bombardment of love will be vulnerable for some reason, which makes them more easily influenced by the excessive attention they receive.

So why would anyone use love bombing in the first place? Often it is because they are needy, depressed, or want to use the other person to help them get what they want. They want to make sure they can use that person by breaking down the walls that stand between them. They will often cause some damage in the process, even if it is because they can form certain types of attachments that are not healthy.

Then there are love bombers who will be considered more sinister. These are the people who will use love bombings as a way to control another person. It will be a ploy with these manipulators to get favor and even some power with a partner and if they don't feel these things towards them. The goal will find that dating these types of people usually doesn't end well. They will get angry or hurt when their partner does not return attention and affection and will never be able to reach the high standards that their partner wants.

As a dark persuader, you may find that working with love bombings can be an excellent practice for you. It allows you to induce the other person to do what you want because they will feel an excessive amount of love on your part. Regardless of whether you think it for your goal or not, that's not the point. You can use it to your advantage to induce others to do what you want them to do.

Disguise true intentions

The next one on the list to watch out for is the idea of masking your true intentions. Sometimes when we are using dark psychology and the different methods that derive from it, it makes more sense when we can hide our true intentions. Maybe it's terrible intentions that the other person won't want to have anything to do with. Maybe hiding our intentions makes it easier to get what we want. Sometimes, even if the end goal isn't all that bad, people won't be happy to find out that someone else is using it, and masking the true intentions ensures you are more likely to get what you want in the process.

There are a few different tactics you can use to help you mask some of your true intentions. Some of the options include:

Use a bait object to help drive the target out of what you are doing.

Your goal with this is to support a cause or some kind of idea that will go against your feelings but will help you achieve your goal. Use this tactic safely and cautiously.

You want to make sure you can hide your intentions by not closing yourself, but be careful not to be too reserved because this will make other people suspicious of you. You can do this by talking a lot about your goals and desires, but not the real ones.

This will benefit you in many different ways. First, it will make you appear open, confident, and friendly to the other person. He will do it

they will help you hide some of your true intentions and send your rivals on a wild goose hunt that will take up a lot of your time.

False security

People will confuse the idea of sincerity with honesty. Remember, most people's first instinct is to trust appearances, and since they appreciate honesty, they will try to believe that there is a lot of goodness in those around them. This means that even if you are only able to show them the idea of honesty, they will want to believe that you will always do it and be honest with them.

Stick to facial expressions that will be tasteless

Behind an insipid and illegible type of exterior, you can overcome all sorts of chaos. And since nobody can read facial expressions and more of what you are giving, you can plan many problems for the other person, without having an idea of what you are doing. This is a weapon that will do you good, so practice some of the mildest body language and facial expressions signs you can find.

Using noble gestures

The next thing you can do is work with what noble gestures are. Remember that people want to be able to trust what you are saying and believe that there is something suitable for all people. They want to think that any kind of gesture that seems noble is something they can trust because this is a pleasant belief. They will rarely take a look at the deception that could happen behind the scenes with this.

Find a way to belong to the group.

People tend to confuse appearances with reality, the feeling that if someone seems to belong to your group, their belonging must be real. This is a habit that will make it easier for a dark persuader to blend in perfectly and have the front they need for their ideas.

The resulting trick will be unaffected. You just need to merge with those around you. The more you can join and appear to be part of the group, the less suspect you will be. Remember that it will take a little patience and maybe a little humility to do it. But it will ensure that you can join the group you need and that others will not harm you in the process.

Tendentious questions

The next option we can consider when it comes to dark persuasion is asking essential questions. A central question will be a question that will contain or imply the answer the persuader wants you to answer. It will make the other person feel as if they need to respond in a certain way if they're going to be right.

Usually, when we ask a question, we do a neutral one. This will be a type of problem that will not suggest your answer, allowing the target to answer in any way they choose. But the main questions will pretty much tell the goal of how they will answer, which is why they turn into a form of persuasion that you need to be careful of. They will be rhetorical in a sense because they will involve answers that can attempt to shape or determine a solution.

Now, this won't always be a hostile question type or one that should put the other person in place. At least not always, instead, it will only say which answer you want the target to use, and sometimes these can be hostile but often if you don't want to put the other mark on guard, and then you won't ask the question in an antagonistic way.

Let's take a look at an example of how it will work. Let's say a seller wants to be able to sell some furniture to someone. It wouldn't help them say something like, "So buy it already. It's just a sofa!" This will drive other people crazy, and they'll go out without making the purchase. Instead, they might say something like, "When will you get your furniture? "Regardless of the response from the customer, this implies that they are moving on with the purchase if they need it right now, or perhaps they are waiting until the end of the month when they move on to get the investment.

The main questions must be used correctly. They must have a friendlier tone so that the person who listens to them does not feel that they have been attacked or give the wrong answer. But they also have to be done in a way that doesn't hide intentions as much. They will push the other person, the target, to make one

the decision, and hopefully, if done correctly, it will work well and to their advantage.

The law of the state of transference

The law of the state of transference is that which the manipulator will use regularly. It allows them to work to get the feeling you feel towards them so they can stay with you. Usually, this will be a transference you weren't planning on, and this can cause a lot of trouble because you give your love and attention to someone who doesn't deserve it, rather than the right person. Sometimes, you realize you are doing it, and you don't know how to stop it; other times, you have no idea, which locks you in a bad cycle from which it is difficult to get out.

First, we need to take a look at the idea of the transference. This will be a psychological pattern in which we will unconsciously experience a person through the filter of feelings towards someone else he had known in our past. Often someone else we are filtering from the past will be someone we knew from our childhood.

Let's take a closer look at how it works. Imagine having a best friend you've known for a long time. And then suddenly this friend starts acting like I'm their bossy father. During this time, notice that the conversations you started sideways. The friend can explode from 0 to 100 in a second and usually on a bribe that has nothing to do with the conversation you two had. You sit there, and you feel that things have gone off course, and you are not sure why.

The problem isn't really about you. This is the idea that the friend went through and worked with the concept of the transference. The anger and other negative feelings they had for the father are now being put on you. This could be a bad thing for your friendship, mainly because you are not that person, and it may be time to step back.

But someone who is using dark psychology may be able to use it to their advantage. It could take some time to learn a little about their goal and maybe find out who the target has loved and lost in the past or someone significant to the destination. So through some secret methods, they will be able to transfer that love and affection to themselves. This is why it seems that the target will fall madly in love with someone new, and want to do anything for that person, even when he doesn't know them.

Historically, when we look at the idea of transference, it will come from the plan that we will practically transfer the feelings we have for one person to someone else. It will often be used, although not always exclusively, about any feelings that may arise towards another person. But it wasn't still like this.

Freud initially used it as a kind of neurological term. But when he was able to write The Interpretation of Dreams, he also used this more as a psychological phenomenon. The turning point was Freud's work with his patient named Dora. The transference in therapy assumed a more significant role because of the work that was shown.

This raises the question of whether or not the transference will be a kind of defense mechanism for the patient. This is believed to be because it will be used to protect the target from any emotional pain they have. However, when we take a look at the neuroscience perspective, the brain often works less mysteriously.

When we look at it this way, this transference will take place when the brain is trying to have a unique experience that it needs to complete its development.

But how the idea of transference works when it comes to the relationship is what is most interesting for someone who uses dark psychology. It is believed that we will all experience a kind of transference to some extent in our relationships. When this happens, we will transfer some of our unsatisfied psychological desires or desires to someone else.

This means that you will experience the person you are having a relationship as if it were just like someone else. And you will react to them that way. This does not mean that you are crazy, even if it is something you should consider working with. Instead, this type of transference will be done to satisfy one of your psychological needs. This may be as simple as you need to end an interpersonal conflict that you have been dealing with since you were a child. It may not be the right way to do it, but that's what the brain is doing.

Additionally, you may find that transference will arise when working with a caring healthcare professional that you, in your subconscious mind, experience the same emotions and attitudes as a loving mother, whether you have had them or not in the past. You will begin to experience the other person in this way because there is a part of you that craves an experience that was missing in the past. The brain will be able to use this as a way of filling the gaps in your story.

Sometimes this is seen as a healthy thing. It helps the brain function properly and deals with some of the developmental stuff that may have been lost in the past. That said, when someone who uses dark psychology tries to use this, it won't work either. This is because they will end up with some problems in trying to make the transference appear where it does not belong, or because they want to keep it longer than necessary to satisfy their needs. They will take a process that should be considered normal and transform it to get what they want from the mix.

As you can see, there are several methods you can use when working with dark persuasion to get what you want out of life. Making sure you use these techniques and choose the right one to work with the goal you choose will make a big difference in the amount of success you are going to find.

Conclusion

The notion that dark psychology is prevalent and that it is part of our world can be a scary thought. The Dark Triad is a term in dark psychology that can be helpful when trying to pinpoint the beginning of criminal behavior.

Narcissism exhibits these traits: egotism, grandiosity, and lack of empathy

Machiavellianism uses a form of manipulation to betray and exploit people. Those who practice this do not practice morality or ethics.

Psychopathy is a trick to those who put their trust in these types of people. They are often charming and friendly. Yet they are ruled by impulsivity, selfishness, lack of empathy, and remorselessness.

The fact that people can be used as pawns on a chessboard makes all of us want to understand dark psychology more and to figure out what it is, and how we can save ourselves from it.

There are many ailments that hypnosis can make better or even cure. And we are not just talking about mental ailments, but physical as well. Hypnosis can be used to help cure some of the side effects that are caused by chemo and radiation in cancer patients.

We all know that there has been a lot of skepticism for this alternative medicine due to the quacks that use it as a laughingstock. However, when used correctly, this type of medicine can do a lot better than harm because it wakes peoples subconscious up to letting go of things that they are holding on to that might be causing a plethora of problems in their lives.

With this being said, all of these methods can be used for good; it is just based on their intentions and the overall outcome. Those who use manipulation tactics do not use them for the intention of helping anyone. Manipulating is changing someone's thoughts, actions, and behaviors to fit someone else's (the manipulator's agenda). There is no way to sugarcoat some of these techniques. And that is why they fall under the dark psychology umbrella because they have been used by criminals to get what they want as well.

Because we all know that someone is going to try to make us a victim of one of these methods again, sometime in our lives, and I for one would want to be as ready as I could possibly be.

There are many examples of manipulation, mind control, and persuasion in history. Some of the most infamous examples are Charles Manson, Adolph Hitler, and Ted Bundy. When you look at Charles Manson, you are able to get a profile of someone who was able to use his words and "love" for his "family" to create a cult. He was able to take young adults and make them into murders. You need to remember that Charles Manson never actually killed anyone. He simply had the members of his "family" do this through manipulation, mind control, and persuasion.

Adolph Hitler was the same way. He started by getting people to like him through persuasion. People believed that he would be one of the greatest political leaders of all time. While he did go down in history, it is not because he was a great political leader.

www.ingramcontent.com/pod-product-compliance
Lightning Source LLC
Chambersburg PA
CBHW071441070526
44578CB00001B/185